D1632390

11.

Date checked

7/8/00

Edition in print

DNE Only in French

Other copies in stock

0

X995 204926 1923 0E

WOLVERHAMPTON PUBLIC LIBRARIES
CENTRAL LENDING LIBRARY

Telephone : 20109 & 26988

Open 10 a.m. to 7 p.m. each weekday

C.14

TO RENEW QUOTE THIS NUMBER AND LATEST DATE STAMPED

712209

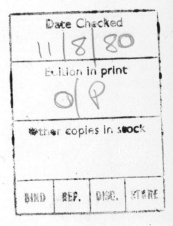

Date Checked

11 | 8 | 80

Edition in print

O/P

Other copies in stock

BIND	REP.	DISC.	STORE

X995 204926 1923 0E

COLOMBE

By the same author:

RING ROUND THE MOON
ANTIGONE AND EURYDICE
ARDÈLE
THIEVES' CARNIVAL

JEAN ANOUILH

COLOMBE

A Comedy

In a Version by
DENIS CANNAN

With a Preface by
PETER BROOK

X 9 9 5 2 0 4 9 2 6 1 1923

METHUEN & CO. LTD. LONDON
36 Essex Street, Strand, W.C.2

WOLVERHAMPTON
PUBLIC LIBRARIES

*This play is fully protected by copyright. All
enquiries concerning the rights for professional
production should be addressed to* TENNENT PRO-
DUCTIONS LTD., *Globe Theatre, London, W.1,
and for amateur production to* DR. JAN VAN
LOEWEN, *International Copyright Agency, 2,
Jason's Court,* 78 *Wigmore Street, London, W.*1

CENTRAL LENDING

Class No. 842ANO

Invoice No. T.

Book No. 712209

Checked

First published in 1952

CATALOGUE NO. 4587/U

PRINTED IN GREAT BRITAIN

TONBRIDGE PRINTERS LTD., PEACH HALL WORKS, TONBRIDGE, KENT.

This play was first presented by Tennent Productions Ltd. at the New Theatre, London, on December 13th, 1951, with the following cast:

MADAME ALEXANDRA, *a famous actress*	YVONNE ARNAUD
JULIEN ⎫ *her sons* PAUL ⎭	MICHAEL GOUGH JOHN STRATTON
COLOMBE, *Julien's wife*	JOYCE REDMAN
EMILE ROBINET, *a dramatist*	ESME PERCY
DESFOURNETTES, *a director of the theatre*	DAVID HORNE
LAGARDE, *an actor*	LAURENCE NAISMITH
MADAME GEORGES, *a dresser*	ROSALIND ATKINSON
SURETTE, *a secretary*	ELIOT MAKEHAM
A HAIRDRESSER	VERNON GREEVES
A CHIROPODIST	BILLIE HILL
A MANICURIST	PENELOPE MUNDAY
JOSEPH ⎫ *stage hands* LEON ⎭	PETER WIGZELL TIMOTHY FORBES ADAM

The play directed by PETER BROOK

ACT 1 .... A Theatre in Paris, 1900.

ACT 2 .... The Same. Three months later.

ACT 3 .... The Same. Three hours later.

EPILOGUE—The first meeting. Two years before.

PREFACE

By Peter Brook

The reaction of a great number of Englishmen, including many serious critics, to all the post-war school of French plays has been one of suspicion and reserve. Their authors' philosophies have been mocked, their view of life dismissed as "cynical" and "pessimistic," labels have been rushed on to the plays as an insulation to preserve us from being gulled by their ideas. Each new French play is treated as a Wooden Horse: critics toil like Trojans to smell out and warn us of the enemy concealed under the benign exterior. For the Frenchman is still the "Frog": in many a London club the Battle of Agincourt is still being fought, the shadow of Boney lurks sinisterly behind the billiard cues: Voltaire's remarks that Shakespeare was a barbarian are still remembered, his little experiment in dissecting a human body to find its soul, is quoted as "typical": what with shades of Edward VII, Emma Bovary and the Moulin Rouge, the Frenchman is still the dangerous foreigner, most likely to undermine when he is most plausible and charming.

For once again, it is the eternal contrast between French logic and the Englishman who is a poet and an idealist, writing sonnets as he pulls the bomb release, and dreaming behind his moustache. His romantic heart is hidden behind his façade, his home is his castle, a castle whose walls the Frenchman bores with his pin. . . .

Every time a play crosses the Channel it loses weight. I am sure of this, though I'm afraid no scientist and no weighing machine could prove me right. But take a French play—a good one, that is, a play that is good not only because of its dialogue, but because of its ideas and characters. Have a translation made—a good one, that is, not a literal one, but

7

WOLVERHAMPTON
PUBLIC LIBRARIES

one that says in a natural English way exactly what they say in the French. Then, by normal schoolboy arithmetic, the two should be equal. But unfortunately this is where life is oddly unscientific; detail for detail the two scripts may be identical, joke for joke they may be the same, and yet somewhere, somehow, a something will have dropped out. In fact the play will have lost weight on the journey.

To find out what has happened we must look at the most fragile part of the play. This is its surface—the words as opposed to the ideas, the jargon as against the characters—for these things give a play a skin as sensitive as the palm of a hand. The most trivial plays may deal with the most unimportant topicalities; the greatest plays may treat deep-rooted problems of life and death; but the author of either will search in the same way for the most vivid means with which to speak his mind. So the words he chooses will instinctively be the words that at the moment of writing seem to carry most weight: he will reach continually into the hidden Stock Exchange where from hour to hour words are endlessly changing meaning and importance, reflecting all the events that pass and the fashions that change.

An author writing in Paris to-day has a stock of words that reflects all his experience of French life. As he writes he may ponder on how to make his notions clear, but he will not think twice about everyday things. He will not think anyone could misunderstand a reference to Dior, or to the Café Flore, he will let a character send a "pneu" without adding a line or two to explain this peculiar way of sending a letter, he will write about the Champs Elysées without thinking anyone could imagine he means the Elysian Fields. The author will be grounded in roughly the same education as a large part of his audience: Shakespeare quoted endlessly from the Stratford-on-Avon Latin Grammar, and the Frenchman quotes from the legends, myths and classical heroes that have been drummed into him at Lycée with the help of Corneille and Racine. He will share many of the same prejudices with his audience, he will have the same

8

sense of humour, he will have many views in common on politics, religion and sex. So as he puts pen to paper the French author will arrange his play in the sure knowledge that there are a great number of points which do not need any form of introduction. It is like dropping in on an old friend, one can get to the point without any of the preambles and courtesies needed for the total stranger. In many cases the French play is difficult to translate because it is based on aspects of French life that the English do not understand: the problem is made infinitely more difficult when it is based on ideas which the French accept without question and which the English cannot swallow at all.

On all these scores a play that crosses the Channel can lose weight, because if the audience is confused or if the audience is hostile, the same scene may have to be expressed in a very different way before it can make the same effect. In fact, to say truly in English what the original author meant to say, a translation is not enough. A "version" is needed. This word "version" is not just a new affectation of the Francophile snob: it covers a rather different and larger task. To make a version the adaptor must first prepare a script full, as it were, of holes. Then out of his own imagination the adaptor has to create material to fill these gaps. In his version of *Colombe*, Denis Cannan has at times strayed a long way from Anouilh's details, though never from his intentions. Word for word, the French and the English *Colombe* vary; idea for idea they are just about the same. Anouilh's aim is to speak through comedy: to woo his audience into swallowing his bitter pill; Cannan's aim equally has been to divert, so that even those most on their guard against the wickedness of cynical and pessimistic Frenchmen can be seduced into forgetting their suspicions in laughter and tears.

ACT ONE

MADAME ALEXANDRA'S *dressing-room, and a corner of
the passage outside. Enter* JULIEN *and* COLOMBE.

JULIEN. If we wait for her here we can't miss her. . . .
That's the door to her dressing-room.

COLOMBE. Shall we see some of the actors, do you think?

JULIEN. We might. They're not much to look at when
they're not on the stage.

COLOMBE. Where is the stage?

JULIEN. Along the passage and down the stairs.

COLOMBE. Could we go and look at it?

JULIEN. Why?

COLOMBE. It was where we first met. . . .

JULIEN. Two years ago. . . . You were a flower girl, and I
was a first year student. We hadn't ten francs between us
—remember?

COLOMBE. Your brother lent us twenty to go and have
supper at Poccardi's.

JULIEN. We must have been mad.

COLOMBE. Why?

JULIEN. Getting married, with less than the price of a
supper to keep us. . . . I never thought I'd have to bring
you back. I never thought that after two years we'd have
no more money than we had on the day we got married.
Colombe, my darling. . . .

COLOMBE. Yes?

JULIEN. I do love you.

COLOMBE. I love you too. . . .

11

JULIEN.   And I'm sorry.

COLOMBE.   What for, my darling?

JULIEN.   Because I haven't any money. Because I can't support you as a husband should, and I have to come begging to my mother. . . . Kiss me, to show you don't blame me. . . .

> *They kiss.*
>
> *Enter* GEORGES. *She looks at them for a moment in surprise before they notice her and break apart.*

JULIEN.   Georges!

GEORGES.   Master Julien! Well, this is a surprise.

JULIEN.   This is Madame Georges, my mother's dresser. Georges, this is my wife.

GEORGES.   Your wife! You've gone and got married?

JULIEN.   Yes. Don't you remember her?

GEORGES.   I can't say I do. She wasn't in the company, was she?

JULIEN.   No. She worked in the flower shop around the corner. Two years ago she brought a bouquet for my mother——

GEORGES.   Of course I remember! They offered her the part of the flower girl in the *Princess and the Beggar*— and she turned it down—and you had a row with the author because he wanted to look at her legs. . . . It was poor Monsieur Robinet, that's who it was—and you gave him such a kick you tore half the seat off his trousers! The best playwright in France, Member of the Academy, Legion of Honour, and he couldn't sit down for a fortnight! Well, to think it's the same girl and you've married her! She's so grown up I'd never had known!

JULIEN.   We've a child now, too . . .

GEORGES.   You have? A boy or a girl?

COLOMBE.   A boy.

12

GEORGES. How old is he?

COLOMBE. He's just a year.

GEORGES (*suspiciously*). How long have you been married?

COLOMBE. Two years.

GEORGES. Three months to spare—that's all right, then. . . . Well, you'd better make yourself scarce before Madame Alexandra comes in. She's in one of her tempers today, and you won't improve it, Master Julien.

JULIEN. But we've come here specially to see her.

GEORGES. O . . . You have, have you? Is it money again?

JULIEN. I've just been called up to do my military service. I want to ask her to look after my wife and child for the three years I'm away.

GEORGES. You don't want much, do you? Three years is a long time.

JULIEN. Do you think I like coming begging for charity? She's the last person in the world I'd ask a favour, but there's no other way. I haven't any money and I can't borrow. I've sold my piano to pay for the baby's winter clothes.

GEORGES. It all comes of you're going in for music. If you'd gone into government service as she told you, you'd have some savings to fall back on——

JULIEN. Georges, my career is my own business.

GEORGES. It's a fine career that doesn't keep your family. Well, you'd better sit down and make yourself tidy and wait till she comes in.

JULIEN. Thank you, I'd rather stand. . . . Where is the old girl? We've been waiting at the stage door for half an hour.

GEORGES. The old girl! That's a nice way to speak of your mother!

JULIEN. I'll call her what I choose. How does she speak of me?

GEORGES. She doesn't. She won't have your name mentioned.

JULIEN. This is going to be a charming interview.

GEORGES. It depends on you, Master Julien. If you keep a civil tongue in your head she might listen. But if you start your rampaging and shouting you'll find yourself out in the street.

JULIEN. I didn't ask for your advice, thank you.

GEORGES. I dare say not. But it wouldn't do you any harm if you took it.

JULIEN. Just stop talking, Georges, will you? It gets on my nerves.

GEORGES. That's right. Start your sulks. He's just like his father was before him, and I wouldn't be surprised if he ended the same way.

COLOMBE. What happened to your father?

GEORGES. Blew his brains out.

JULIEN. Georges!

COLOMBE. You never told me. What happened?

GEORGES. His father was a colonel in the army. He fell in love with Madame when we went to Morocco on tour. She put up with him for two weeks, and then she left him for the juvenile lead.

COLOMBE. You mean—he killed himself?

JULIEN. Father was a man who took life very seriously. He entered himself as dead on the regimental records, wrote a requisition for one cartridge, and shot himself while reading the epistles of St. Paul. Now you know. . . . How much longer shall we have to wait?

GEORGES. I've been waiting for Madame Alexandra for thirty years, and I've never known her to be punctual yet. Thirty years I've been sitting and waiting. When I undress you can see the marks of the chain.

JULIEN (*taking her by the shoulders*). Georges, if you don't stop talking I'll brain you.

GEORGES (*calmly*). Two years since he saw his mother, gets

14

married without a word to anyone, comes in here just before rehearsal and in five minutes he's knocking me about. . . . Have you seen his brother?

COLOMBE. No.

GEORGES. Different as chalk from cheese. If you want a welcome from your mother, you'd better learn some manners from Master Paul. He knows how to make himself agreeable. And stop treading on her train! Look at it! And I've just ironed it for this evening!

JULIEN. What part is she playing?

GEORGES. *The Empress of Hearts*—worst play of the season. Five quick changes and a pompadour wig. Give me the *Sister of Mercy*, that's what I call drama. Just one change in the interval: she starts as a nun and ends up as a choirboy.

JULIEN. Look, dear old Georges—it's nearly three o'clock. Would you be an angel and go down and see if anyone else has come for this rehearsal?

GEORGES. No, I won't. Go yourself. I've some work to do in the wardrobe. If you had any sense you'd go home and write to her. She's used to begging letters—she gets twenty or thirty a day.

She goes.

JULIEN. *The Empress of Hearts*. . . . that makes things worse.

COLOMBE. Why?

JULIEN. She can never attend to family matters unless she's playing a mother at night. In this she plays a beautiful adultress of seventeen.

COLOMBE. Do you really think she'll help us?

JULIEN. It won't be easy; but she has a duty to her family, just as I have a duty to my country. Oh, don't worry. I'll get round the old girl somehow.

15

COLOMBE. It's horrible to speak of her like that! After all, she is your mother.

JULIEN. You want me to call her "Dear Mumsy" like my brother? Oh, I'd be glad to—if she'd ever given me any reason for affection.

COLOMBE. Why's she so fond of your brother, and not of you?

JULIEN. Because Paul was the son of a jockey, who was the only man she ever really loved. He was the youngest, the nicest looking, and he reminded her of the pleasures of the turf. He was always the favourite: he was kept at home, exhibited at parties, photographed on her knee for all the smart magazines. . . . I was boarded out at a baby farm in the country. Once or twice a year she paid me a visit—just to make sure I was alive. My mother didn't want me, and my father shot himself before I was born. For all the parental affection I've had, I might as well be an orphan.

COLOMBE. My poor darling . . . (she kisses him). But now you needn't be alone any more. You've got me to love you and look after you——

JULIEN. Only till tomorrow. Tomorrow I'll be alone all over again, polishing buttons in the camp at Chalons.

COLOMBE. But I'm sure that if you ask your mother really nicely, with all her influence she could get you excused your service.

JULIEN. I don't want to be excused! Do you think I'm the sort of person who'd fake an illness or pull strings to get out of doing my duty?

COLOMBE. Not for yourself, perhaps. But . . . wouldn't you do it for me? Three years! It's such a long time——

JULIEN. Colombe, my love—I've no one but you. You know how miserable I'll be at leaving you, but how could you love me any more if I did something cowardly simply to stay near you?

16

COLOMBE. My darling—how silly you are! Don't you know that I'd still go on loving you whatever you did?

GEORGES *rushes in.*

GEORGES. She's coming! She's stopped at the stage door to sign autographs for some students.

JULIEN. Haven't they harnessed themselves to her carriage yet? When she has a success it's a tradition: they take out the horses and she gallops home with half the university in the shafts. And she's so mean that she's seriously considered whether she couldn't spare herself the expense of keeping horses.

GEORGES. If you go on this way, Master Julien, it'll be just the same between you as before——

JULIEN. I shall go on exactly how I choose——

GEORGES. Men! They're all the same. I'd better go and warn her you're here. . . .

She goes.

COLOMBE. Julien—you know you've got to ask her a favour. Please be nice to her—please just be polite. For my sake—and for your son's sake. . . .

Distant applause, and MADAME ALEXANDRA'S *voice.*

JULIEN. Just listen! D'you hear it? Trotting out the old stage door performance she's done for forty years, puffing and blowing like a fat old sow snuffling for anything they'll throw her. Oh, it's obscene! On the stage she's Juliet, Isolda, Helen, Cleopatra! She smiles and simpers like a painted little girl . . . and she's my mother.

COLOMBE. Julien!

JULIEN. Are you ready to make your pretty curtsey to the Queen of Love? Prepare to be blinded by her beauty—it's dazzled three generations!

COLOMBE.   I'm frightened.

JULIEN.   Of her? Don't worry—she doesn't bite. She lost her teeth long before she lost her lovers. And the famous pet panther you may have heard of—he was so eaten by moths they had him destroyed.

Enter MADAME ALEXANDRA *with her retinue;* GEORGES, SURETTE, *a hairdresser, a manicurist, a chiropodist. She passes* JULIEN *and* COLOMBE *without a glance and stalks towards her dressing-room.*

MME. ALEXANDRA.   My son, you say? Useless! Inform him that I do not wish to see him.

The dressing-room door closes behind the procession.

JULIEN.   Oh no! This is too much! This time I'll smash down the theatre!

COLOMBE.   Julien, be sensible! You won't get anything by shouting!

JULIEN.   Let me go. I shall shout as much as I like. If I don't shout I shall burst. Mother!

He rushes into the dressing-room and beats at the door of Madame's sanctum.

Mother! Let me in! Let me in, or I'll break down the door!

He does his best, but the door is a solid one.

Ah! Locked out, am I? The loving son might get his fingers in her purse. . . . Madame Alexandra! Leave me out here and your vases will be in pieces! I'll make off with your bronzes, Madame. I'll put a foot through your bogus Botticelli! Open the door! I'm much cheaper than the furniture, Madame! Open, will you! (*He shouts even louder, shaking the door.*) Madame Alexandra, you're wanted on stage! It's the great scene with the prodigal

18

son! For one last time you can play the Ideal Mother! comic c
Your public is waiting—your entrance has come!

> *The door is opened by the* CHIROPODIST, *who holds it firmly.*

CHIROPODIST. Madame has asked me to say that she is unable to receive you. She regrets that she has a rehearsal.

JULIEN (*through the half-open door*). Madame Alexandra, I am perfectly calm. I am quite astoundingly calm. But I have no intention of discussing family matters with your chiropodist. Will you please do me the favour of granting your son a personal interview.

MME. ALEXANDRA (*a shriek through the door*). Tell him to go out of my room and wait in the corridor!

JULIEN. Very well, Mumsy. I will wait in the corridor— Mumsy. . . .

> *He goes out, slamming the door. He comes face to face with* COLOMBE, *who has been waiting in great perturbation.*
>
> *The* CHIROPODIST *has hurried to shut the door.* GEORGES *comes out of the inner room, and as she slips into the passage, the* CHIROPODIST *turns the key behind her.*

GEORGES. Well! That's got you a long way, hasn't it? Didn't I tell you to be nice to her? How do you expect people to swallow a pill unless you give it with something sweet?

JULIEN. I've nothing sweet in my constitution.

GEORGES. You don't need to tell me that. . . . But show a bit of good nature, Master Julien—butter her up a bit——

JULIEN. Why should it all be on my side? It's two years since I've seen her. A nice welcome I got!

GEORGES. You didn't expect her to kill the fatted calf, did

19

you? Whenever you come here it's always for money. It's as bad as having bailiffs in the house.

> *During the last remarks* MME. ALEXANDRA *has come into the outer room in her dressing-gown. She enthrones herself majestically while the* CHIROPODIST *takes her foot, the* MANICURIST *her hand, and the* HAIR-DRESSER *her head.* SURETTE, *her secretary, stands respectfully waiting with a sheaf of papers in his hand.*

MME. ALEXANDRA.   Surette!

SURETTE.   Madame?

MME. ALEXANDRA.   I will attend to to-day's correspondence.

SURETTE.   Certainly, Madame. Benoiseau has sent his account respecting the costumes for the Empress. It is the third reminder.

MME. ALEXANDRA.   Tell him to wait.   Next?

SURETTE.   A request from the stage hands: they are asking for a rise of six francs a month.

MME. ALEXANDRA.   Refused. Next?

SURETTE.   The Society for the Relief of Consumptive Students requests a gift for their charity bazaar.

MME. ALEXANDRA.   I sent something to the students last week.

SURETTE.   But these are consumptive students.

MME. ALEXANDRA.   Either they are students or else they are consumptives—they must really make up their minds!

SURETTE.   They point out that Madame Sarah Bernhardt has sent them one of her own pieces of sculpture.

MME. ALEXANDRA.   Point out to them that I do not puddle about in clay like Madame Bernhardt! I save my energies for the theatre!

SURETTE.   Madame Bernhardt's little present has caused quite a sensation. . . .

MME. ALEXANDRA. Madame Bernhardt never does anything without causing a sensation. How large is the piece of sculpture?

SURETTE. If it is the terra-cotta clown which she exhibited recently, I don't think it is much larger than that, Madame.

MME. ALEXANDRA. Is that all? I'm surprised at her. Georges!

GEORGES (*in the passage to* JULIEN). She wants me. Now stay where you are. Everything'll be all right—you trust me.

She goes in, opening the door with her pass key and locking it behind her.

Yes Madame?

MME. ALEXANDRA. What have you done with that atrocious bronze someone gave me two years ago and we could never find room for?

GEORGES. The woman without any clothes on, Madame?

MME. ALEXANDRA. No, not the nude, you idiot! That nude is by Rodin. They needn't imagine they're going to get a Rodin out of me, just because they think they've got consumption. Besides, it's a scientific fact that everyone has consumption. I read it somewhere. I can't think what they're grumbling about.

GEORGES. Ah—I know the one—the skeleton holding someone in its arms.

MME. ALEXANDRA. Yes, that's the one.

SURETTE. *The Young Man in the Arms of Death.* We put it up in the attic.

MME. ALEXANDRA. Send it, with my card. It is three times as large as the terra-cotta clown, and that will infuriate Madame Bernhardt.

SURETTE.   But . . . it might be thought, Madame, that the subject was a little . . . *The Young Man in the Arms of Death*—for consumptive students?

MME. ALEXANDRA.   They can take it or leave it—it's all I have! And if they are consumptive they know perfectly well that they're going to die, don't they? Really, you'll all drive me mad!

JULIEN (*who is getting restive in the passage*). If she thinks she can keep me waiting all the afternoon, she's mistaken.

COLOMBE.   Julien—do be sensible!

JULIEN (*beating on the door*).   Mother!

> *Everyone in the dressing-room is transfixed, waiting for their cue from* MADAME.

MME. ALEXANDRA.   Next?

SURETTE.   A young man from Toulouse, who writes that he has seen you in *The Empress of Hearts* and that he would willingly die for you.

MME. ALEXANDRA.   How kind. Thank him. Next?

JULIEN.   Mother—open the door!

MME. ALEXANDRA (*in a shriek*).   Next!

SURETTE.   A letter from your son, who says that he will come to see you this afternoon in the theatre. He says that it is urgent.

MME. ALEXANDRA.   Next?

JULIEN (*kicking the door furiously*).   Mother! I shall go on kicking this door until you open it!

MME. ALEXANDRA (*to* SURETTE).   Did you hear me? I said next!

SURETTE.   Um . . . the Fire Brigade, Madame.

MME. ALEXANDRA (*exploding*).   The Fire Brigade!!! What does the Fire Brigade want with me? We haven't a fire, have we? Tell them that they also can wait until I send for them.

SURETTE. It is their annual charity fête, Madame. . . .

MME. ALEXANDRA (*the last straw*). Charity! It's always charity! All these people think of is begging for alms! Do I give annual charity fêtes in aid of myself? I began my career in the theatre at thirteen, and since then not a day has gone by but I've given a performance—and I've never asked for a single sou from anyone!

This is punctuated by rhythmic kicks at the door.

JULIEN. Madame Alexandra! If you leave me out here for another hour there won't be a scrap of paint from the floor to the ceiling.

COLOMBE *does her best to restrain him. He thrusts her away and beats on the door like a madman.*

Good God, I'm your son—your son! Your flesh and blood—your son!

COLOMBE (*tearing him suddenly away from the door*). Julien! That's enough! I hate you like this!

JULIEN (*stopping at once—staring at her amazed*). Oh? You hate me too? I see. I won't say anything more.

He sinks into a chair with his head in his hands.

MME. ALEXANDRA (*breaking the unnatural silence*). Next?

SURETTE. What shall I say to the Fire Brigade? Madame Sarah Bernhardt has sent them a hundred francs.

MME. ALEXANDRA (*beside herself*). If Madame Sarah Bernhardt has money to throw away, I have not! I don't go on tours round South America like a circus! Send them flowers. Send them all the flowers I've been given this week.

SURETTE. Flowers? For the Fire Brigade? . . .

MME. ALEXANDRA. Yes! Are you deaf!

SURETTE. It's only that some of your bouquets are rather wilted now, Madame.

23

MME. ALEXANDRA. Very well—they can spray them with their hoses—excellent training.

She rises.

And now that is quite enough. I am perfectly exhausted. We will deal with the rest of the post after the rehearsal. I must go and attend to my make-up.

SURETTE (*bowing obsequiously*). Exactly as you wish, Madame—exactly as you wish.

SURETTE *withdraws.* GEORGES *opens the door for him with her pass key, and makes a sign to* JULIEN *to be patient.* MADAME *has gone into the inner room, attended by her staff.* GEORGES *follows them.* SURETTE, *alone in the passage with* JULIEN, *drops his mask.*

The old bitch!

JULIEN *glances up at him.* SURETTE *resumes his humility.*

I mean to say that she's sometimes rather difficult.

JULIEN. You're right.

SURETTE. And it's been like that every single day for the last ten years, cringing there beside her with my papers in my hand. . . . Yes, of course, Madame. It will be as you say, Madame! It will be attended to, Madame! And what do I get in return? A vase thrown at my head. "Surette, you're a stupid old ass!" she'll shout—just loud enough for everyone to hear. And I must go down on my knees to pick up the vase—but careful! I must keep the smile on my face. Dear Madame is so eccentric, so amusing. All must be forgiven to such genius.

JULIEN. Why do you stay with her?

SURETTE. Because, like all stupid old asses, I have a fancy for my fodder. I like to fill my stomach twice a day. And as it's she who brings the nosebag to my stable, I swallow the thistles for the sake of the good green clover. I imagine that you're here on an errand for a similar purpose. Am I right?

JULIEN.   Oh, go away—you're too disgusting.

SURETTE.   But it's she who made me so. To cringe is in my contract. Well, it's your turn now. Run along in and be nice to mamma. Oh, we're all the same—we puff out our chests and stand on our principles, and then one fine day we're down in the dust with our pretty pink tongues licking our master's boots. Oh yes, dear Madame, I'm a stupid old ass and I know it, but even old asses must bray for their feed . . . bend and bray . . . bend and bray . . .

He goes.

JULIEN.   He's filthy. Filthy and disgusting. Come—we'll go!

Enter PAUL, hurrying to the dressing-room. He stops, staggered to see JULIEN.

PAUL.   Julien! Good heavens—where on earth have you sprung from? And—who's this?

JULIEN.   My wife. . . . This is my brother Paul.

PAUL.   Is this the little flower girl? And you've really married her? Old Julien, a married man—congratulations! But where have you been all this time—America?

JULIEN.   Belleville. Near the gas works.

PAUL.   And—have you been working?

JULIEN.   I've been giving piano lessons. Luckily gas workers aren't very musical.

PAUL.   And you've come here to make things up with mother? Let me see what I can do to help.

JULIEN.   No, I don't think so. We were just going.

PAUL.   Leave it to me, and I can promise you a splendid reconciliation.

25

JULIEN. No. It's very good of you, but we must go.

PAUL. Are you . . . short of cash? I'm afraid I was cleaned out last night—never had a card in my hand. But if I go in and have a word with her, I'm sure everything will be fixed in no time——

JULIEN (*stopping him*). No. I just called in as I was passing. She's busy. We're perfectly all right. It's nice to have seen you again.

He tries to lead COLOMBE *away, but she escapes him and runs to* PAUL.

COLOMBE. Sir, don't believe him! He's just being proud. He came here to try to see his mother——

JULIEN. Colombe!

COLOMBE. I *will* tell him! We've got a child, sir—and Julien has to go and do his military service. He came here to ask her if she'd look after us when he's away.

PAUL. A child?

COLOMBE. Yes. Last year.

PAUL. And you'll leave this poor little thing all alone to bring up a child without a franc in her pocket? Is that what you've come to tell mother?

COLOMBE. Yes, sir. And as she wouldn't see us the moment we arrived, he wants to walk off without a word——

PAUL. But surely you can arrange things, can't you? *I'm* not doing any military service.

JULIEN. I only asked for deferment until I'd finished at the College of Music. I'm leaving tomorrow for the camp at Chalons.

PAUL. Dear old Julien—he's always the same—his principles are so high his head's never out of the clouds! You poor little thing—does he make you very unhappy?

COLOMBE. I love him, sir.

26

PAUL. I'm afraid you do. Yes—we all love him. But that doesn't stop us from thinking that life is very much easier to live than he makes out! So if I hadn't dropped in to see mother, off he'd have gone to wave the flag and save his country! Well, the answer's simple enough; we must set to work and get him exempted.

COLOMBE. You see, Julien!

JULIEN. I'm very grateful . . . but I'd sooner do my duty.

PAUL. Oh yes! That's all very nice and noble and patriotic —for you! But what about her, left all alone to bring up a child and try to make ends meet on a private's pay? What's she going to do with her evenings? Gaze at the magnificent panorama of the gas works of Belleville? You talk about your duty; haven't you a duty to her? Well, if you can't look after your own family, I'll do it for you. If we can't get anything else, we'll get the rent out of mother, and then you can go off with a clear conscience to defend us all from invasion. So much loveliness must have a name. What is it?

COLOMBE. Colombe, sir.

PAUL. Colombe! It's a wonderful name! Where did you find it?

COLOMBE. It's the name of a saint.

PAUL. Oh, what a pity. I thought it had been invented specially for you. But I'm sure she couldn't have been a real saint—a saint, shall we say, with some redeeming sins. . . . Now follow me, the blushing bride—with all the charm you can muster. But I don't think I can teach you much about charm, can I?

COLOMBE. Oh, yes, sir. I'm very shy with strangers.

PAUL. You don't say so! And you mustn't call me sir— my name is Paul.

By now they are in the outer room. COLOMBE *looks at the furnishings in amazement.*

27

A pretty little nest, our mother's, don't you think? All newly done up in the reigning style: everything perfectly in key—and utterly bogus. Why don't you sit down? (*He indicates a divan covered with skins*): Careful! Treat it with respect! The lion skin was given her by an English Duke. He shot the lion in Africa and himself in the Ritz. Mother thought of asking for his skin, too, but he had to be buried in Westminster Abbey. Mumsy, darling, how are you?

He has gone into the inner room. COLOMBE *is alone.* JULIEN *peers in from the passage.*

JULIEN. Has he gone in to see her?

COLOMBE. Yes. How kind he is! How happy and gay! You see how right I was to tell him?

JULIEN. Yes.... Listen, Colombe: I'm going to leave you all by yourself.

COLOMBE. Yes.

JULIEN. The world's a much harder place than you believe.

COLOMBE. I know.

JULIEN. I want you to . . . to try to grow up a little, and take life more seriously.

COLOMBE. Yes.

JULIEN. If you don't, you'll become one of Mother's kind of people: never happy without pleasures.

COLOMBE. I know. You've explained it before.

JULIEN. It's the world of pleasures you'll see now. It'll all seem so new, so dazzling——

COLOMBE. Yes.

JULIEN. But it's all false, my darling—you must realise that.

COLOMBE. Yes, I'm sure.

JULIEN. I know that you listen to what I tell you, and that you'd never do anything wrong on purpose; but you've

28

never met this kind of people before. You might so easily be misled.

COLOMBE (*with a giggle*). You mean that I must be very careful?

JULIEN. Yes. Will you promise to be as careful when I'm away as you would be if I were here?

COLOMBE. Of course I'll promise! But . . . you don't mind if I enjoy myself a little, do you?

JULIEN. It depends. There are right and wrong sorts of enjoyment.

COLOMBE. Suppose . . . just suppose some gentleman tells me that I'm pretty, and offers to buy me a posy of flowers. Is it wrong if I accept them?

JULIEN. I think it would be safer to refuse.

COLOMBE. Even if I don't give him anything in exchange?

JULIEN. Perhaps, but . . . I shall be a long way off, and I shan't be able to advise you. If you really love me . . .

COLOMBE. But of course I love you, my darling!

JULIEN. If you knew how much I need your love just now. . . . Well, if you love me. . . . Are you listening?

COLOMBE. Yes.

JULIEN. You're not looking at me.

COLOMBE. No. But I'm listening.

JULIEN. If you really love me, you'll try to give me all your love, not just a part of it. You'll have no love left for these other things you love.

COLOMBE. No love left for flowers, or necklaces, or dresses? Mustn't I love to look in shop windows and pretend I'm rich enough to buy anything I see?

JULIEN. Not if you really love me.

COLOMBE. But I don't expect you to buy me the things I like. I only want to . . . look, and pretend.

JULIEN. You shouldn't want to look when you know that I can't afford to buy you such things.

COLOMBE. It makes life rather difficult . . .

JULIEN. Life *is* difficult—that's what I'm trying to tell you. Now, will you promise to do as I wish?

COLOMBE. Living with you is like being back at school, and always being frightened because one hasn't done one's homework.

JULIEN. Colombe, you're my wife. You promised to take me for rich or poor, for better or worse. Didn't you?

COLOMBE. I said so.

JULIEN. You promised.

COLOMBE. In that stuffy Town Hall in front of the Mayor, with his nose dripping on the Register? Did that count as a promise?

JULIEN. You promised afterwards in church. Oh, I know that the old priest gabbled the service so fast we thought he must be in a hurry to get it over. Perhaps God was in a hurry too. But you made the promise, my love. Will you make it again to me now?

COLOMBE. All right, I promise. There! Are you happy?

JULIEN. Cross your heart.

COLOMBE. I cross my heart. . . .

JULIEN. And . . . if you have to see Paul again, you won't get too fond of him, will you?

COLOMBE. But he's been so kind.

JULIEN. That's exactly why I'm warning you: the kind people are often the cruellest—just as I'm sometimes cruel to be kind.

COLOMBE. Oh, how difficult everything always is with you! I have to think six times before I dare to open my mouth. And to me, it all seems so simple. Everyone's kind and doing their best; and all I ask of life is . . . a little happiness . . . just happiness. . . .

Enter PAUL.

30

PAUL. Victory! What are you doing here?

JULIEN. Talking to Colombe.

PAUL. Well, you'd better make yourself scarce. I want to get her used to the idea of Colombe first. You can come on in the second scene—erring son, forgiving mother—we only need to give her the cues and she'll play it perfectly. Oh—I haven't broken it to her yet that she's a grandmother. At her age the news might kill her. We'll announce it gently later on, with some delicate circumlocution. You agree? It doesn't outrage too much your sense of rectitude?

JULIEN. Thank you, Paul. It's very good of you to take all this trouble——

PAUL. Nonsense! There's nothing good about me, and you know that as well as I do. And the only trouble will be if she finds you here. Go on—wait in the corridor. (*He closes the door behind* JULIEN.) Now: I shall bring the dragon in here when she's ready. And stand up to her— look her in the eye! Like all bullies, she's secretly a coward. Don't be scared—I'll hold your hand. . . .

> *He goes into the dressing-room.* COLOMBE *is all alone among the tapestries and vases and ferns and potted palms.* JULIEN *is all alone on the hard chair in the passage on the other side of the wall.*
>
> DESFOURNETTES, *Madame's partner in the direction of the theatre, comes down the passage with* ROBINET, *the playwright: two fur collars, two top hats, two canes, four whiskers.*

DESFOURNETTES. Wonderful, my dear fellow! Wonderful!

ROBINET. You think so? Really?

DESFOURNETTES. I congratulate you upon a work of genius. Of genius! I have racked my brain, and I can think of no other word adequate to describe it.

ROBINET. Genius will do perfectly well . . . just as long as you think that I've earned my keep. . . .

DESFOURNETTES. The last act will be a sensation. (*Passing* JULIEN.) Excuse me. . . . (*He notices him.*) But— Julien, is it you? You dear dreadful boy—what are you doing here?

JULIEN. I'm waiting for my mother.

DESFOURNETTES (*perturbed*). Does she know you're here?

JULIEN. Paul has gone to break it to her.

DESFOURNETTES. Because we simply can't have any unpleasantness before the rehearsal, you know. Why don't you come back at six? We open on the twenty-second, and we haven't a minute to lose—you ask Robinet. (*He notices* ROBINET'S *expression.*) My dear fellow, what on earth's the matter?

ROBINET. I am waiting.

DESFOURNETTES. What for?

ROBINET. An apology.

DESFOURNETTES. What apology?

ROBINET. This young gentleman will no doubt inform you.

DESFOURNETTES (*suddenly enlightened*). Ah! Of course! That little matter of assault and battery. But that was two years ago. Surely it's all forgotten and forgiven by now?

ROBINET. Not yet.

DESFOURNETTES. Julien, couldn't you pocket your pride and make an apology? I'm sure that by now you've both forgotten what the quarrel was about.

JULIEN. I haven't. Far from it.

DESFOURNETTES. Oh, how tiresome you are! Robinet, can't you make the first move? I've had plenty of experience in delicate affairs of this kind, and he didn't slap you in the face, he merely kicked you. I assure you that an

32

assault with a lower limb is not technically an insult to the recipient's honour.

ROBINET. Do you recollect *where* he kicked me?

DESFOURNETTES. On the stage, wasn't it?

ROBINET. And . . . (*He lifts his coat tails.*)

DESFOURNETTES. Oh. In that case it was an insult. Julien, dear boy, now couldn't you make a generous gesture?

JULIEN. If I make a gesture it certainly won't be generous. It'll be in the same direction as the last.

DESFOURNETTES. Oh, why must you be so difficult? I'm sure that Robinet did nothing serious to annoy you! And you, dear fellow, couldn't you by stretching a point assume that he kicked you rather lower down? Now I come to think of it, I remember distinctly that it was the *leg* of your trousers that was torn. There was no damage to the seat whatever.

ROBINET. There was considerable damage to *my* seat.

DESFOURNETTES. Oh, accidentally, no doubt——

ROBINET. No! He *aimed* at the seat.

DESFOURNETTES. Oh, I'm sure he didn't. (*To* JULIEN.) Now, just to put everything right, all you've got to do is to assure our old friend that you never took aim at the target he imagined.

JULIEN. I did. And I'm heartily glad I scored a bull's-eye.

DESFOURNETTES. Oh, you're impossible! I've finished with you. Come along, Robinet.

> ROBINET *passes* JULIEN *with great dignity, but his walk betrays an anxiety for his unprotected rear.* DESFOURNETTES *stops suddenly as he sees* COLOMBE.

DESFOURNETTES. Oh! Good afternoon. Are you waiting for Madame Alexandra?

COLOMBE. Yes, sir.

ROBINET. Charming! But she's perfectly charming! Mademoiselle, surely we've met somewhere before?

COLOMBE. Yes, sir. Two years ago. Down on the stage.

ROBINET. (*involuntarily clapping a hand to his rump*). Oh, yes—of course . . . and you were with—— (*He glances towards the passage.*)

COLOMBE. That's right, sir. . . . And now—he's my husband.

ROBINET (*icily*). My congratulations.

DESFOURNETTES (*at the door of the dressing-room*). Are you there, dear lady? Our poet has finished the new ending, and it's brilliant—a work of genius!

ROBINET (*simpering with rapture*). Oh, please, don't exaggerate. I've just done my little task to the best of my ability.

Enter MME. ALEXANDRA *in her stage costume. She is followed by* PAUL, GEORGES, *and her staff.*

MME. ALEXANDRA. Where is this child? Pretty . . . very pretty. . . . Dear Poet!

ROBINET. Dear, dear Great One!

They fall into each other' arms.

MME. ALEXANDRA. My own, own Genius! To think that such a dear sweet person should be the poet of his age! To think that he's such a great, great god, and I have him under contract! Have you slept well, my precious treasure?

ROBINET. Slept, dear lady, when Art is calling?

MME. ALEXANDRA. Ah, yes, Art—of course . . . your cruel mistress who has worn you to a shadow—my poor precious, he's quite pale with composition! A chair! A throne for my Poet!

A bustle. A chair is placed for ROBINET *and another is moved for her.*

No! Not for me—what right have I to be seated in the presence of my sovereign? Place me a pouffe at his feet.

ROBINET (*rising*). Dear lady, I cannot allow it! To you and your genius I owe all!

MME. ALEXANDRA. Oh, you good, good, perfect man! My archangel—return to my arms.

They embrace again.

The greatest of poets, and the silly doesn't know it!

ROBINET. Queen of the Stage—Queen of our Hearts!

MME. ALEXANDRA (*ending the scene abruptly*). Come on—two chairs, two chairs!

They sit. She looks at COLOMBE.

This child is a perfect princess. She must have her hair done differently, of course. . . . Dear poet—I am all attention.

ROBINET (*taking the manuscript from his pocket*). This comes after the big scene in the last act—when Gitana has chosen to die.

MME. ALEXANDRA. I remember the moment. She is reclining, pale as death, on a chaise longue. All in white—thirty yards of chiffon—splendid, splendid! I see it completely.

ROBINET. I will begin: "O moon so wan, my heart's chill friend in death——"

MME. ALEXANDRA. Superb! Beautiful beyond belief. "My heart's chill friend in death". I know exactly how I shall say it.

She has never stopped looking at herself in the mirror. Suddenly she shouts:

Lucien!

HAIRDRESSER. Madame?

MME. ALEXANDRA. Look at this! You've made me look

like a poodle. Arrange it at once. And afterwards you can do your best with that idiot girl. Dear poet—pray continue.

ROBINET. "O moon so wan, my heart's chill friend in death . . ."

MME. ALEXANDRA. That's very good. Really very good indeed. Lucien, you're hurting.

HAIRDRESSER. This is the false hair, Madame.

MME. ALEXANDRA. I don't care what it is—you're hurting! Proceed, dear poet.

ROBINET. "O moon so wan, my heart's chill friend in death,
Shall I thus share with thee my spirit's gall?"

MME. ALEXANDRA. That is far better.

ROBINET. You—you didn't like the first line?

MME. ALEXANDRA. I meant my postiche. Both lines are delightful. "Shall I thus share with thee my spirit's gall?" At that moment I shall stretch out my hand in a kind of astronomical supplication. The moon should be downstage left. And we need a new one.

ROBINET. "Shall I thus share with thee my spirit's gall?
Unloved is she who dared to love too long!
In her bruised heart black hatred bars the doors . . ."

MME. ALEXANDRA. "Black H-a-tred bars the doors!" It's *very* good—so true, so exactly like life.

ROBINET. "And Love lies sickly sweet upon his bier
To rot in odours, like the trampled rose.
O too fond heart, can'st thou not find some path
Without this wilderness of tangled thorns?
No hand to take thy bleeding fingers' clasp . . ."

MME. ALEXANDRA (*rising and patting him as she passes*). But it's magnificent! A torrent, a flood, an inundation of genius! Lucien! I will tell you what to do with this child.

36

Face the light, you little silly. You will sweep all this back, and take this low down on the neck—so. Perfect. Who bought you this ridiculous dress?

COLOMBE. Julien, Madame.

MME. ALEXANDRA. I might have known it. He has as much taste as his father. Go on, my dear poet, go on—I am listening. "No hand to take thy bleeding fingers' clasp . . ." You see, I know my lines already. Georges, pass me my jewels. The false ones. . . . In five minutes, little savage, you won't know yourself.

ROBINET. "No hand. . . . No hand. . . ."

> *He is unable to secure attention, and*
> *continues for his own lugubrious satis-*
> *faction:*

> "No hand to take thy bleeding fingers' clasp,
>   And lead thee where the meadows blush with
>   flowers?"

MME. ALEXANDRA. Beautiful! Such feeling! Such cadences! Paul, what do you think of her now?

PAUL. I wouldn't know her. You're a fairy godmother.

MME. ALEXANDRA (*still admiring* COLOMBE). Why don't you wear any jewels, you dowdy little goose? They suit you so well.

COLOMBE. Because I haven't got any, Madame.

MME. ALEXANDRA. Neither had I at your age. But I had the sense to save them from the Christmas crackers. They were false, but they sparkled just the same.

COLOMBE. Julien doesn't like false jewellery.

MME. ALEXANDRA. Don't mention that nincompoop to me! How have you put up with him for two whole years? I left his father in two weeks. . . . A person who doesn't like false jewels should set to work and earn enough money to buy real ones, instead of going off to earn

37

soldier's pay and leaving his wife to other people's charity. Lucien, take her away! Georges, find her something to wear! Paul, you know how to dress up a woman— you can take charge. Dear poet, your work is wonderful— the apex of your genius. . . . But I wanted to ask you something. You know who this child is?

ROBINET.   Yes, dear lady, I do.

MME. ALEXANDRA.   Julien has to do his military service. Of course, I could have him excused; the Minister for War could hardly refuse me a favour—I refused him none. . . . But, there it is, Julien wants to go. Well, the girl must work. I can't support her. I wondered if we couldn't employ her by putting in just a few little lines at the end of the last act. She speaks quite well, and we could make her a Muse or something——

DESFOURNETTES (*suddenly exploding*).   Here! No! I see what you're after! You want to get her supported by the management. No, thank you. Oh, no!

MME. ALEXANDRA (*raging*).   Will you be quiet! You're a nobody—a little worm in the office who does what he's told!

DESFOURNETTES.   I am co-director of this theatre! I'm a business man and I won't hear of it! Great God, you've got enough money to look after your own family, haven't you? You take thirty per cent of the gross as it is!

MME. ALEXANDRA.   Brute! Swine! Throw him out! Never let me see him again!

DESFOURNETTES.   The play is cast. There are thirty-two characters and sixty costumes—we'll never cover our costs as it is!

MME. ALEXANDRA.   You think of nothing but money! It's disgusting. And I go down on that stage and every night I half kill myself for the public—I pour out my life's blood for my art!

38

DESFOURNETTES. Pour it out free of charge, and I'll be very grateful!

MME. ALEXANDRA. Free of charge! You presume to insult me? Very well . . . I feel my migraine coming on. I cannot rehearse.

DESFOURNETTES. Now, really . . . dear Madame . . . we open on the twenty-second. We can't cancel the production now! And *The Empress of Hearts* is losing money every night. . . . My dear old friend, it's four o'clock. Everyone has been waiting for you on the stage since half-past two. Come down and rehearse. Please. . . . I give in. I will engage the girl.

MME. ALEXANDRA. Seven francs a performance. Double for matinees.

DESFOURNETTES. But—that is absurd! If she's only saying four lines, the salary rate is——

MME. ALEXANDRA. Then we'll write her twelve lines, that's all! You're a tradesman, Desfournettes, a dirty shopkeeper! I really don't know why we consent to be seen with you.

DESFOURNETTES. Oh, very well, then. Seven francs—even for four lines, even if the Muse is dumb. But come down and rehearse—please, I implore you!

MME. ALEXANDRA. Dear poet, your new ending is perfectly superb.

ROBINET. But I've only read you a few lines——

MME. ALEXANDRA. That doesn't matter—I can foresee the rest. And you *will* be a dear friend and add me a little something for the child, won't you? We can audition her after the rehearsal. Lucien! This is superb! Now I no longer look like a poodle, I look like a seal! What have you done with it, you fool?

HAIRDRESSER (*rushing to her assistance*). But, Madame, you've disarranged it yourself.

MME. ALEXANDRA. Ass! Idiot! I could kill you. But I've no time now. . . . Dear poet, your last act is wonderful! But do you know what I would suggest?

ROBINET (*anxiously*). No—what?

MME. ALEXANDRA. If I were you, I should cut the first six lines.

ROBINET. But you only listened to the first seven.

MME. ALEXANDRA. Exactly. Begin with the seventh: "O too fond heart, can'st thou not find some path?" It gets to the point without wasting time.

ROBINET. But that will leave out my line about the trampled rose.

MME. ALEXANDRA. I will have real roses. That will be far more effective than trampled ones.

ROBINET. But my vowels, dear great one—as only you can speak them: "O moon so wan——"

MME. ALEXANDRA. I will begin, "O too fond heart . . ."

ROBINET. "My heart's chill friend in death . . ."

MME. ALEXANDRA. "Can'st thou not find some path . . ." *(Together.)*

They go out together, both reciting at the tops of their voices. GEORGES comes out of the inner room and runs into the passage.

GEORGES. Everything's all right, Master Julien. She's got round the manager and your wife's going to work in the theatre. And it's all thanks to Master Paul. . . .

JULIEN. Do you mean she's going to act?

GEORGES. Of course! The author's giving her four lines at the end and she'll get seven francs a day. So you can go off without a care in the world. . . .

JULIEN. Am I allowed in now?

GEORGES. Master Paul's just helping her to try on a dress. Seven francs a day—and double for matinees. . . .

She goes. PAUL *comes out of the dressing-room.*

PAUL. I'll see you tonight, then. And you look—wonderful. Wonderful!

He meets JULIEN *in the door.*

Go in, old boy—you won't know her! Now I must dash. Georges has told you? Everything's as right as rain. Shall I see you tonight?

JULIEN. I don't think so.

PAUL. Then good luck—have a nice game of soldiers, and don't worry about her. She'll be well looked after, I promise you.

He hurries away. JULIEN *goes into the outer room.* COLOMBE *comes in, beautifully dressed, bejewelled, transformed. She runs to the glass.*

COLOMBE. Julien! Julien—is it really me?

JULIEN. Yes, it's you. I recognise your voice, anyway.

COLOMBE. If you knew how funny they all are! They all talk at once, they scream, they fight, they fall in each other's arms! Oh, I'll never be bored with them! And I'm going to act! I'm a Muse with four whole lines! I shall have a dress specially made for me—and it isn't all sometime soon, it's now, tonight, tomorrow! (*Turning and preening before the glass.*) Oh, Julien—is it me? Is it me?

JULIEN. Is it my wife? Colombe, I don't know any more . . .

COLOMBE (*forgetting him, forgetting everything in her ecstasy at the glory of her reflection*). It's me! It's me! It's really, really me. . . .

CURTAIN

41

ACT TWO

SCENE 1

*The stage of the theatre: trees, fountains, hampers, paint pots,
dimly lit by a single working light.* JOSEPH *is painting
some scenery. Enter* MADAME ALEXANDRA.

MME. ALEXANDRA.   Is no one here?

JOSEPH.   Not yet, Madame Alexandra. They must have
thought the rehearsal was at half-past two.

MME. ALEXANDRA.   Well, put on some lights. And fetch
my chair!

JOSEPH (*going into the wings*).   Lights! Lights for Madame!

> *The lights are switched on.* JOSEPH *and* LEON *bring an
> imposing chair.* COLOMBE *enters shyly.*

MME. ALEXANDRA.   Has *no one* come in yet?

LEON.   I haven't seen anyone, Madame.

> JOSEPH *and* LEON *go into the wings.*

MME. ALEXANDRA.   So they think they can keep me
waiting while they sit over luncheon and guzzle their
greasy slops. . . . They can't act, and they're late for
rehearsal, and then they come crawling for a rise. . . .
Lazy, lagging, loafing, lecherous muck!

> *Suddenly she sees* COLOMBE.

Oh, is it you, my child? I was dreaming . . .

42

COLOMBE. I think I'm a little bit early, Madame. The rehearsal isn't until half-past two.

MME. ALEXANDRA. I try always to arrive a little early if I can—just to gossip with the shadows, to commune with the virgin canvas of this vast unpeopled stage. . . . I muse, I dream. . . .

COLOMBE. I'm so sorry, Madame—I must have disturbed you. . . .

MME. ALEXANDRA. Oh, never mind **now**. I have mused enough. Can you play poker?

COLOMBE. No . . .

MME. ALEXANDRA. Pity. We could have had a game while we wait for those swine to finish lunch. I know what we'll do—we'll tell your fortune. Come along—cut the pack. Ah, what a lucky girl you are to have all your future before you.

COLOMBE. Is that better than to have a great past behind you?

MME. ALEXANDRA. Perhaps not. But a great past is always yapping at one's heels . . . one, two, three, four—clubs! Excellent—that means money. News of a fair young man . . . a little affair, agreeable, but very soon over—those are the best. . . . More news of the fair young man.

COLOMBE. But Julien is dark.

MME. ALEXANDRA. What's that got to do with it? You don't have your fortune told to get news of your husband. The post is sufficient for that. Cut again. The king of hearts and the ten of clubs together. . . . You will marry a man who is very rich and successful.

COLOMBE. But I've got a husband . . .

MME. ALEXANDRA. My dear child, I have had seven. You will get a divorce. Congratulations. Another club.

COLOMBE. You've been married seven times? Really properly?

MME. ALEXANDRA. Of course properly! What do you take me for? In my position it is necessary to marry one's lovers. There was even one I married twice. A sugar king. Once when his mother died, and again after the death of his father.

COLOMBE. You married him—to console him?

MME. ALEXANDRA. No. To share his inheritance.

Enter SURETTE.

Ah, there you are, you old fool. This is a fine time to arrive!

SURETTE. But the rehearsal isn't until half-past two, Madame.

MME. ALEXANDRA. All right—I know, I know. . . .

SURETTE. I've just been working on your interview, Madame.

MME. ALEXANDRA. What interview?

SURETTE. The editor of *Figaro* wants to know what you think about love.

MME. ALEXANDRA. Oh, they'll drive me mad, always wanting to know what I think. Do I ask the editor of *Figaro* what *he* thinks?

SURETTE. Apparently Madame Sarah Bernhardt has given them a very full reply, Madame.

MME. ALEXANDRA. A fat lot Madame Sarah Bernhardt knows about love. What has she said?

SURETTE. She has said that she doesn't believe in it, Madame.

MME. ALEXANDRA. Then tell them that I do believe in it—from the very bottom of my heart. Tell them it is for love alone that I have lived.

SURETTE. I made so bold as to write something on precisely those lines, Madame. I will read it over: "Love, that has swept each generation on its tide; love, that with its

44

name alone brings blushes to the purest cheek; love with a capital L, our brittle hearts' first care . . ."

MME. ALEXANDRA. Buffoon! Idiot—nincompoop—ass! Do you want to make me a laughing stock?

ROBINET *has entered*.

Dear poet! My saviour! Come to my rescue! That wretched *Figaro* can't go to press until it knows what I think about love.

ROBINET (*kissing her hand*). What insolence—and how superfluous. Tell them that you *are* Love!

MME. ALEXANDRA. I can hardly say that to them myself. Dear old friend—find me some witty thing to say!

ROBINET. Of course—what could be easier? Um . . .

> "All have I given. Giv'st thou me
> Unto death the all of thee.
> Twixt us twain shall surely be
> Tum-te-tum eternitee."

A moment . . .

He takes out a notebook.

MME. ALEXANDRA. But not in verse—they'll never believe it's by me!

ROBINET. Oh yes, of course. Let me think. . . . "Love is giving—the gift of self . . ."

MME. ALEXANDRA. Perfect, perfect. Take it down, idiot!

ROBINET. "But all that one gives is for oneself."

MME. ALEXANDRA. It's very profound. But don't you think a little bitter?

ROBINET. The truth is always bitter, dear lady. Should we conceal it?

MME. ALEXANDRA. But I want to show them my faith in the Ideal! Compose me a clarion call to youth and beauty!

ROBINET. Oh, very well. Delete. New page.

"That love's rare bloom may fertile flourish
  All that which weeds and tares doth nourish . . ."

MME. ALEXANDRA. Not in verse!

ROBINET. I beg your pardon—I forgot myself. Delete. New page. "That love may flourish in the good earth of our souls it behoves the prudent husbandman diligently to root from his heart the rank weeds of passion and desire." How's that?

MME. ALEXANDRA. But what are you saying? How can love possibly exist without passion and desire? Why, when I was not a day older than this chit of a girl I had already died of love on four separate occasions! And can you—you, with your sensibility—tell me that you have never suffered?

ROBINET. Like a dog, dear lady—like a dog!

MME. ALEXANDRA. And I too! Oh, I've been mad—I have driven others to the very doors of delirium! Did you know that one Christmas Eve at the circus I drove dear Salvator-Dupont to break into a cage full of lions to prove his passion? How he adored me! (*To* COLOMBE.) You're a woman, my little one. Just imagine how it was. You have said no to this man. You love someone else—you know how it is, you can't oblige everyone. A sudden cry. He leaps from his seat and rushes like a madman into the middle of the lions. There is a great shriek from the audience. You cannot help it—louder than all the rest you cry "I love you!"

ROBINET. Wonderful! That shriek in the arena—I hear it now! (*To* SURETTE.) Take it down, take it down!

MME. ALEXANDRA. "I love you! Return! I give my all!" Too late.

COLOMBE (*wide-eyed with amazement*). He was eaten?

MME. ALEXANDRA. No. He came out. And once he was

out of the cage I loved him no longer. His only hope was to have possessed me there and then among the lions, and that was too public to be possible.

COLOMBE.   Oh, how I love listening to you! It's all like something in a book. But what does one have to do to get oneself loved as you were?

MME. ALEXANDRA.   Be a woman, my dear, that's all. For dull, drab beings be everything they think beyond their reach. Then, like little boys, they'll be driven to do anything just to catch your attention. One day at Maxim's when I had no appetite—I lived only on Art and champagne in those days—I was slimming—dear Salvator, beside himself because I wouldn't eat, ordered them to bring him a raw rat, and he devoured it there and then before my eyes.

ROBINET.   Madness! Beautiful, sublime madness!

COLOMBE.   And so—you ate something then, just to please him?

MME. ALEXANDRA.   I? It was revolting. I could hardly keep down my champagne. I slapped his face and walked out. And the cream of the joke was that they brought him a bill for fifty francs for the rat.

ROBINET.   Wonderful woman! Who is there but you to tend the flame of beauty and romance—to light for us all one last shimmering corner in this base material world? Incidentally, I meant to ask you—have you anything in the Panama Canal?

MME. ALEXANDRA.   I think so.

ROBINET.   Sell. Sell at once. In the next week they'll drop ten. And you know what to buy?

He leads her away, whispering.

Russian bonds. Russian. You can make thirty francs each if you buy now.

47

MME. ALEXANDRA. And the three per cent?

ROBINET. Steady—perfectly steady. Have you bought anything in armaments?

MME. ALEXANDRA. No. Do you believe there will be a war?

ROBINET. There always is, if one waits long enough. Now I'll let you into a secret I heard only the other day . . .

They are departing.

SURETTE. But what shall I tell them you think about love, Madame?

MME. ALEXANDRA. Oh, tell them anything you like! Can't you see that we're talking about something important?

They go. GEORGES *has shuffled in with a dress over her arm.*

SURETTE. And tomorrow they'll publish a reply by Rejane, and it'll be I who'll get the blame for it.

He goes.

GEORGES. It's no good interrupting them when they're talking about money. We'll be lucky if we start the rehearsal before three. Ah, it's a life and a half, the theatre. Can't call your soul your own. And how are you liking it, now you know what it is?

COLOMBE (*lost in her dream*). Oh, very much, thank you.

GEORGES. You don't think it's a better life to sit at home of an evening darning your husband's socks and waiting till it's time to lift the baby?

COLOMBE. No . . .

GEORGES (*she looks at* COLOMBE *for a moment, then shrugs her shoulders*). Oh, we're all the same. We grumble and grouse, but we've got it in our blood, that's the trouble. I must go and have a look at her costume. Last night the President was in front. She curtsied so low at the calls she burst her bodice.

> *She has gone.* LAGARDE *makes a great entrance: wide-brimmed hat, an elegant cane, a flower in his buttonhole: youth eternal, tinged with grey.*

LAGARDE. Ah, good afternoon, my little one. Are we the first?

COLOMBE. No, Madame Alexandra is up in her dressing-room.

LAGARDE. Oh . . . she's demn punctual for a change, our great lady. I dropped in early on purpose to have a chat with you. How's the work going?

COLOMBE. Madame says that I'm improving.

LAGARDE. Yes, you show great promise—a little stiffness as yet, but the promise is there. . . . You should come along to my place after a rehearsal some evening. I'd give you a little private coaching.

COLOMBE. Would you really, Monsieur Lagarde?

LAGARDE. A drop of port, nibble a biscuit, gossip about this and that—just pot luck, y'know, in a bachelor's den. Quite a snug little place I've got—had it done up all oriental. (*He comes closer.*) You little devil, I'm mad about you. Last night I never closed my eyes.

COLOMBE. Oh, but you mustn't miss your sleep, Monsieur Lagarde.

LAGARDE. How can I sleep when nothing will make me forget you? Drink is useless, drugs ineffective, Swedish exercises only make me worse! This morning I was found by my valet stretched in a coma on the hearthrug, crying out in delirium, "Colombe, Colombe!"

COLOMBE. You have a valet? All to yourself?

LAGARDE. A Turk I imported from the steppes of Arabia —giant of a man in a crimson turban—why don't you come and see? He will serve you like a Sultana, not a word will pass his lips. . . .

COLOMBE. Is he dumb?

LAGARDE. Dumb? Like all Orientals he knows *when* to be dumb. We will dress too like a Sultan and his slave . . .

COLOMBE. But Monsieur Lagarde, I hardly know you.

LAGARDE. What d'you need to know me for? Isn't it enough that I exist? Come and sample the pleasures of the East and I will teach you what it means to be a woman. . . .

COLOMBE. I think I should know best about that, Monsieur Lagarde. But how have you managed to fall in love with me so quickly?

LAGARDE. Because I have awaited you so long.

COLOMBE. Have you? Really?

LAGARDE. Of course!

COLOMBE. But . . . you see, Julien loves me too.

LAGARDE. As I do? Does he roll on the ground, does he groan?

COLOMBE. It would be rather difficult if a husband behaved like that. . . . But Monsieur Lagarde, suppose that when I came to see you I had no appetite. Would you, just to encourage me, devour a raw rat before my eyes?

LAGARDE. A raw rat? What on earth for?

Enter DESFOURNETTES.

DESFOURNETTES. Ah—afternoon, Lagarde.

LAGARDE (*coldly*). Good afternoon.

DESFOURNETTES. You know that you're supposed to be rehearsing in costume? Madame is dressed and ready.

LAGARDE (*with a black look*). I'm going. Are you coming up to change, too, dear?

50

DESFOURNETTES. She doesn't come on until Act Five—
she's plenty of time. And I want a word with her—on
business.

LAGARDE. M'm—well, ·this evening, perhaps? All the
pleasures of the East, you know—ha-ha!

He catches DESFOURNETTES' *eye and is suddenly
deflated.*

Yes. . . .

He goes.

DESFOURNETTES. After the rehearsal just look into my
office, will you? A drop of port, nibble a biscuit . . . and
we'll sign your contract. I know I made a bit of a fuss the
other day, but that was only for form's sake. Don't
worry—you'll get your seven francs. Would it help
you at all if I let you have a little something in
advance?

COLOMBE. Oh yes, sir—it would.

DESFOURNETTES. Drop in, then, and we'll see what we
can do. Tell me, is it true that you've nothing to wear but
that one dress?

COLOMBE. Yes.

DESFOURNETTES. Oh well, we must do something about
that! I know a dressmaker who gives me a discount. What
would you say to a little outfit for the spring—I believe
what they call Vieux Rose is the thing this season. I can
just see you all in Vieux Rose, with a touch of fur round
the . . . throat.

COLOMBE. Oh, but if you really mean it, what I'd much
rather have would be a nice little fur cape with a fur bonnet
to match. I saw a lady wearing that in the street this
morning—it looked so becoming! And perhaps I could
have a little fur muff to match the cape and——

51

DESFOURNETTES. Yes, yes. . . . A dress with some fur trimming. We must see about it . . . sometime.

Enter ROBINET.

ROBINET. Where, where, *where* is my little Muse?

DESFOURNETTES (*icily*). She is here. With me.

ROBINET. Do you know, dear fellow, that I simply can't live without her? And the dear little poppet has positively inspired me! Last night I wrote her six extra hexameters! There stands before you, you exquisite child, a man who hasn't closed an eye since yesterday—all because of you!

COLOMBE. You too?

ROBINET. What do you mean—I too?

DESFOURNETTES (*sharply*). Look here, Robinet, the play's long enough as it is. Don't start adding any more.

ROBINET. Oh, do be quiet! She has great talent, and I personally will give her a little coaching. Now if you'd like to come along to my place after the rehearsal—a drop of port, nibble a biscuit—I'll send a cab for you . . .

DESFOURNETTES. After the rehearsal? She can't—she has an engagement.

ROBINET. She can cancel it, can't she? We open on the twenty-second. Work must come before pleasure, you know!

DESFOURNETTES. She has to sign her contract. That's work, isn't it?

ROBINET. If it's one of your contracts it certainly won't be a pleasure. Well, it won't take a second—trot along up and do it now.

Enter PAUL.

DESFOURNETTES. But the contract isn't drafted yet. . . .

ROBINET. Desfournettes! We are in a hurry. We open on the twenty-second, and she has an important part. After the rehearsal she comes back with *me* . . .

DESFOURNETTES. She does *not!* She comes with me!

PAUL (*who has been listening with amusement*). Gentlemen, I will settle the argument. After the rehearsal she has a fitting at the dressmaker's. As there is scarcely time for the dress to be finished for the opening, *I* will escort her after the rehearsal. (*He looks, smiling, from one to the other.*) That is, if you really do want to open on the twenty-second?

DESFOURNETTES. Very well. . . . I shall see you to-morrow, then . . . my dear . . .

He goes.

ROBINET. I must say I think it's the limit. Everything seems to come before the play!

PAUL (*very affably*). Robinet—mother wants you.

ROBINET. I have just this moment left her.

PAUL. She thinks that your new ending is too long.

ROBINET. Too long! For the last week they've done nothing but mangle it! There's only four lines of it left!

PAUL. She's made up her mind that she only wants to say the last.

ROBINET. Only the last? Just one line? But it won't make sense!

PAUL. Then you'll have to make it make sense—that's what you're here for.

ROBINET. This is too much! Who do they think is the author of the play? I won't have my name on the bills. l just won't! We'll see if they open on the twenty-second—we'll see!

He goes.

COLOMBE.   Oh, how dreadful! Whatever will happen?

PAUL.   You don't know the theatre. Nothing will happen—except that he'll cut as he's told. I was only creating a flurry to drive those two elderly moths away from the flame. Do they amuse you?

COLOMBE.   What?

PAUL.   Men.

COLOMBE.   They'd be more amusing if they didn't all try the same tricks. I'm rather tired of complaints about insomnia.

PAUL.   Who's had insomnia?

COLOMBE.   Neither Monsieur Lagarde nor Monsieur Robinet have closed an eye all night.

PAUL.   And Desfournettes?

COLOMBE.   He slept. But he offers me an advance of salary and a spring outfit in Vieux Rose.

PAUL.   And have you chosen between them?

COLOMBE.   Yes. For the spring outfit.

PAUL.   I mean between the donors?

COLOMBE.   Only one has suggested anything useful. The others offer me sleepless nights and drops of port.

PAUL.   And the worst of them all makes the best offer? Yes, that's always the way. Well, it's lucky that I'm here to protect you.

COLOMBE.   To protect me from what?

PAUL.   Their intentions.

COLOMBE.   Oh, there's nothing wrong with their intentions. They only want to coach me in my part.

PAUL.   Is that the best excuse they can find?

COLOMBE.   It's the same one as you found.

PAUL.   Mine . . . was genuine. And the proof of it is that I didn't offer you any port.

COLOMBE.   So I noticed. And I was dying of thirst all the evening.

54

PAUL. I kept my eyes on the script, my hands behind my back, and you at the far end of the dining-room. Oh, I'm not a Puritan, but a glass of port sitting side by side with you on a well upholstered settee . . . well, I couldn't answer for the consequences.

COLOMBE. I don't understand what you're talking about.

PAUL. But I do . . . very well indeed. When I amuse myself, no one does so better. But when I'm responsible for the family honour, I keep my trust.

COLOMBE. As I've got my fitting this evening and I can't come and practice with you as usual, do you think— instead of talking nonsense—we might have a little rehearsal before the others come along?

PAUL. Let's begin. I have the script—I'm never without it.

They arrange chairs.

COLOMBE. Does it bore you to keep on hearing me?

PAUL. Frightfully.

COLOMBE. If it bores you so much, I could always ask Monsieur Lagarde. I don't think it would bore him at all.

PAUL. No, I'm afraid it wouldn't. Come on, now, let's do the bit that went wrong yesterday, and then we'll run through the whole scene.

He sits. COLOMBE *stands beside him.*

COLOMBE. "And if I say, sir, that I truly love you?"

PAUL. "If you say so, sweet maid, can I believe?"

COLOMBE. "And if I say, sir, that my heart doth pain me?"

PAUL. "Your eyes deny your heart, so you deceive."

COLOMBE. How can you tell what my eyes are saying if you don't look at me?

PAUL (*rising and taking her in his arms*). I'm sorry. Now I'm looking.

55

COLOMBE *returns his glance, then turns away with a tantalising modesty.*

COLOMBE. "Ah, sir, I pray you look not thus upon me:
  To know my secrets is to give me shame . . ."
PAUL. "Shame cannot be when true love loves with honour:
  You play with fire and now you fear the flame."
COLOMBE. "A flame that other eyes have never lighted . . ."
PAUL. "A flame that burns us both—can you deny?"
COLOMBE. "Deny I cannot: I am thy creation. . . ."

Her head falls on his shoulder.

PAUL. "What I have made is mine . . . until . . . we die."

He looks for a moment at the little head on his shoulder. Then he speaks in a voice that is suddenly changed.

Then . . . they kiss. (*Reading his script at arm's length over her head.*)
  "To horse! To horse! Tonight I reach Versailles:
  Tonight I make petition of the King!
  Tonight tonight——" etcetera, etcetera. . . .
COLOMBE (*without moving*): Was that better than yesterday?
PAUL (*lifting her head*). You little witch. . . . Where have you learned so much?
COLOMBE. I just say it as I feel it. Acting isn't so difficult as all that.
PAUL. Not for you, perhaps. . . . Was it . . . did you have to think yourself in Julien's arms to say those lines so well?
COLOMBE. Oh, no! The old silly—he'd never say things like that!
PAUL. In the arms of Lagarde, then, perhaps?
COLOMBE. No. . . .

56

PAUL. And you only thought of yourself as Colombe, just as you are?

COLOMBE. Yes. But another Colombe, who loves the person in the play as it says in the script.

PAUL. And when we come to rehearse the scene of farewell, will you really feel unhappy?

COLOMBE. Not really. But the tears will come into my eyes just as if it were life.

PAUL. Has Julien ever made you cry?

COLOMBE. Now and then.

PAUL. When you have to be sad on the stage, do you think of some time when Julien made you sad?

COLOMBE. No. Because one was real life, and the other's —just acting.

PAUL. But whether it's acting or life, the same tears wet your pretty little cheeks?

COLOMBE. Yes. . . .

PAUL. So the same little drops of salt and water can be true one day and false the next?

COLOMBE. I suppose so.

PAUL. Are you quite, quite sure that you always cried the true sort of tears for Julien?

COLOMBE (*on her guard*). Why do you ask that?

PAUL. Just to learn, my little one. I find it difficult to believe that this useful gift of crying to order was an advantage you never used. . . .

COLOMBE. "And if I say, sir, that I truly love you?"

PAUL. "If you say so, sweet maid, can I believe?"

COLOMBE. "And if I say, sir, that my heart doth pain me?"

PAUL. "Your eyes deny your heart, so you deceive."

COLOMBE. "Ah, sir, I pray you look not thus upon me:
          To know . . . my secrets . . . is to give me shame."

He takes her in his arms.

PAUL. "Shame cannot be . . ." You devil. You dirty little
devil. . . .

After a while he lets her go.

All the same . . . we mustn't be too unkind to Julien . . .
must we?

*They stand side by side, and neither dares to look at the
other.*

CURTAIN

ACT TWO

SCENE 2

The back-stage passage and COLOMBE'S *dressing-room.*
     JULIEN *is pacing up and down. He wears the uniform
     of a private soldier.* GEORGES *is working. For a while
     there is silence.*

JULIEN.   Which is her dressing-room?

GEORGES.   Number seven.

JULIEN.   I went home and there was no one there.

GEORGES.   What d'you expect, coming back without any
     warning?

JULIEN.   She pays the people next door to look after the
     baby.

GEORGES.   Looking well, is he?

JULIEN.   I didn't go in. I wanted to see him with
     Colombe. . . . She didn't even come back for anything to
     eat.

GEORGES.   I expect Master Paul's taken her out to a
     restaurant.

JULIEN.   Paul? Does she go out with him, then?

GEORGES.   Now and then. Sometimes it's him, sometimes
     one of the company. How much leave have you got?

JULIEN.   Twenty-four hours.

GEORGES.   How long is it since you went away?

JULIEN.   Oh, just about three months.

GEORGES (*watching him*).   You'll be due for your first
     week's leave quite soon then?

JULIEN. Yes.

GEORGES. Why did they give you twenty-four hours?

JULIEN. "Urgent Personal Affairs."

GEORGES. There's nothing urgent about your affairs is there?

JULIEN. Yes!

GEORGES. What?

JULIEN. If you must know, I've had a letter. . . . A letter about Colombe's behaviour.

GEORGES. Oh . . . (*trying to seem casual*) who wrote it? Someone in the theatre?

JULIEN. Yes.

GEORGES. It wouldn't have been that Surette, would it?

JULIEN. Why do you ask?

GEORGES. He's got a name for that sort of thing, that's all.

Enter SURETTE.

SURETTE. Ten minutes, please!

GEORGES. Ten minutes? Madame's not in yet, and neither's the girl.

SURETTE. That's no concern of mine. I concentrate on doing my job. I don't go gallivanting off to dinner parties at Maxim's. Ten minutes, please! (*He sees* JULIEN: *his face changes.*) Oh! This is a surprise. Have you got leave, then?

JULIEN. Yes. As you see.

SURETTE. A soft time you have of it in the army now. Not like it was in my day. . . . (*Slyly.*) So you've just come back to sniff the theatrical wind, eh?

JULIEN. Yes. (*After a pause.*) I've had your letter.

SURETTE. Have you? Already?

JULIEN. Yesterday evening.

SURETTE. How rapid the posts are nowadays. One would hardly believe it.

60

JULIEN. Thank you for writing.

SURETTE (*avoiding his eye*). Oh, just to keep you in touch. Theatrical gossip, and so on. . . .

JULIEN. Can you spare me five minutes? We could go outside for a drink.

SURETTE. I can't manage it now. I'm understudying, you know. I have to go on for a fellow who's broken his arm.

LAGARDE (*calling down passage*). Georges!

GEORGES (*hurrying*). Yes, Monsieur Lagarde!

> LAGARDE *appears through the door of his room in underpants and a burnous. He is making up.*

LAGARDE. Just come and do me up behind, will you? Is our little Colombe in yet?

GEORGES. Not yet. But I've a nice surprise for you. Master Julien's here—back on twenty-four hours' leave.

LAGARDE. Oh, damnation!

> GEORGES *shuts herself into the dressing-room with* LAGARDE. JULIEN *has listened to their remarks. Now he clutches* SURETTE *by the lapels.*

JULIEN. Is that her lover!

SURETTE. Now now—there's no need to be violent.

JULIEN. Who is he? Can you give me his name?

SURETTE. Not yet.

JULIEN. Who does she usually go about with?

SURETTE. Ah—that's what I like to see! Method in all things. At the moment there are four.

JULIEN. Four!

SURETTE. Possibilities—not certainties. Your brother Paul, Lagarde, Robinet and Desfournettes. All the best kind of people, you see; that is, if we leave out the hairdresser, who attends her just a little too often. . . . He is,

61

of course, attractive to women; a muscular torso—that counts, you know.

JULIEN.   Five, counting the hairdresser. . . . I shall thrash the lot!

SURETTE.   You can do that, of course, but it won't solve anything. You still won't know which of them it is. That's the trouble about having a wife who's . . . prone to infidelity—you never know which of them it is.

JULIEN.   Don't worry. I shall find out.

SURETTE.   How?

JULIEN.   I shall question her.

SURETTE.   Do you think she'll tell you?

JULIEN.   If she won't, I shall question them.

SURETTE.   All five?

JULIEN.   Yes.

SURETTE.   And what about the sixth, the seventh, and the eighth?

JULIEN.   Who are they?

SURETTE.   The ones you'll begin to suspect after you've questioned the first five. . . . Oh, there's no end to it now, my young friend. Once it's happened it can happen again; and with anyone—literally anyone—that's the trouble. Never assume that the man who attracts your wife will necessarily seem agreeable to you. That's rule one. Oh, no! It may be just a voice on the telephone, a photograph, in a drawer, a letter in a strange handwriting. . . .Who? Who? Who? You'll never stop asking yourself that question now. When she buys a hat—who's it for? When she sings in the bath—who's it for? The rouge on her cheeks, the scent behind her ears—for whom does she take all this trouble? Not for you. Oh, no—that's long past, the time when it was you she was after. It's all for some mysterious Monsieur X. Perhaps you know him, perhaps you don't. But from now on, my dear boy, he's going to be by far

and away the most important person in your life. Ssh!
There's someone coming! Perhaps it's her!

They hurry into COLOMBE'S *dressing-room.*

JULIEN.   What shall I do?

SURETTE.   Hide yourself, of course. That's the second rule
of the game—see without being seen.

JULIEN.   Where?

Voices grow nearer.

SURETTE.   Where do you think? In the cupboard—that's
the tradition.

He opens a cupboard and pushes JULIEN *inside. He shuts
the cupboard, tears into the passage and shouts:*

Ten minutes, please! Ten minutes to curtain rise, please!

MADAME ALEXANDRA *has entered, followed by her
staff.*

MME. ALEXANDRA.   Don't yell at me like that, you fool!
The curtain will go up when I'm ready and no sooner. Are
you playing again tonight?

SURETTE.   Yes, Madame.

MME. ALEXANDRA (*disappearing into her room*).   That
will be a treat for us.

Enter COLOMBE, *running.*

COLOMBE.   Where is he? Where is he?

She looks into her room, sees no one, and runs out again.

Georges! Georges! Where's Julien?

She returns to her room and sees JULIEN, *who has just
come out of the cupboard.*

Where have you come from?

JULIEN.   The cupboard.

COLOMBE.   What were you doing in there?

JULIEN.   I was just playing a joke on you.

COLOMBE (*hugging him to suffocation*).   Oh, darling, darling! How lovely, lovely, lovely to see you! What years and years it's been!

JULIEN.   Years and years. Longer than you'll ever know.

COLOMBE.   And how wonderful you look in uniform—my darling, anyone would think you were a general!

JULIEN.   Not quite yet. But there's always a chance. Blue suits me.

COLOMBE.   Have they made you march miles and miles? Sit down—do sit down—you must be so tired, you poor lamb. (*She sits on his knee.*)   How far do you have to march in one go?

JULIEN.   About twenty-five kilometres.

COLOMBE.   Twenty-five! And on the way back do they let you take a tram?

JULIEN.   No.

COLOMBE.   And you have to do all your own washing and mending? Oh, how I'd laugh to see you! And I suppose you haven't had even the littlest bit of time just to think about me?

JULIEN.   Yes. I've thought about you every minute of the day.

COLOMBE.   So you say! . . . But I bet that when you're all being boys together you never think of anything but telling dirty stories. Oh, my love! Night after night all alone, miles apart in our separate beds. Did yours seem very empty and large?

JULIEN.   A military bed is designed for one soldier. And how's the brat?

COLOMBE.   Who? Oh—he's ever so well. They say he'll be talking any minute and he's got four more teeth. How do you like my little spring outfit?

64

JULIEN. Very pretty.

COLOMBE. It's what they call Vieux Rose. Very fashionable this season.

JULIEN. It must have cost a lot.

COLOMBE. No—no, hardly anything. I go to a dressmaker who gives me a discount, and I pay her off by instalments. Besides—I didn't tell you—I've had a rise! Soon I'll be sending you postal orders to spend on your sprees with the boys. You'll be able to buy drinks for the girls you pick up—oh, I know you!

JULIEN. I can promise you that there aren't many girls to pick up in the camp at Chalons.

COLOMBE. But you have late passes until midnight, don't you? I'm quite sure that you've deceived me a dozen times over—now don't deny it, because I just won't believe you!

JULIEN. All the same, I haven't. (*Quite naturally.*) And you?

COLOMBE. Me? Don't be so silly! Even if I'd wanted to, do you think I've had the time? Oh, I've been working myself to death. Are you going out in front? You'll see me being very grand—I'm a Marquise—you'll never know me. It'll put me off dreadfully knowing you're there. Oh, my love! My darling love—how lovely to see you! And you're looking so handsome and well!

JULIEN. Yes.

COLOMBE (*kissing him and getting up*). It's almost worth being kept apart because it's so nice to be together again. Do you mind if I undress? We're going up any moment and I'm ages late.

She goes behind the screen. Garments fly over as she undresses.

How many days' leave have you got?

JULIEN. Twenty-four hours.

COLOMBE. Only twenty-four hours? Can't you tell them that you missed the train?

JULIEN. No.

COLOMBE. Oh, but my darling, that's just dreadful! Because this evening I've got to go out to supper with some very influential people—I can't explain it all now, but it's awfully important—and all tomorrow afternoon I'm rehearsing.

JULIEN. You won't be able to have supper with these people—that's all.

COLOMBE. Oh, but I must! All my future depends on it!

JULIEN. So does mine. All twenty-four hours.

COLOMBE. Now, please, darling, don't be silly! You'll have lots more leaves, but if I don't go to this party it's a chance I might never get again. It's being given by some terribly high up people who may get me a job at the Folies Bergères. Oh—it's all right—I shan't be naked. They want someone of exactly my type to recite some satirical verses. I should be wearing yards and yards of ermine and mink and have only one bare leg. Now you can't mind me showing one leg, can you? And they must have somebody rather special, because the girls who are good at wriggling their bare tummies simply can't speak verse.

JULIEN (*leaping up and shouting*). Will you not speak of such obscenities! Tonight you will give up this supper party and come home with me!

A short silence behind the screen.

COLOMBE. Of course, I might have known that within five minutes of being back you'd be shouting at me.

JULIEN. Yes, I'm shouting! I'll shout as much as I like! And I'll smash up the whole theatre sooner than have things go on like this!

66

COLOMBE *appears from behind the screen in her petti-coat.*

COLOMBE. Go on like what, my darling?

JULIEN. You know perfectly well. Don't try to look innocent.

COLOMBE. But I don't know at all. What do you mean?

LAGARDE *comes half dressed from his room and knocks playfully at* COLOMBE'S *door.*

LAGARDE. Is there anyone ee-in? Are you there, my little puss-puss? I wanted to tell you to be very careful because —because your husband is . . . (*On opening the door he confronts* JULIEN.) Oh, I beg your pardon.

JULIEN. Not at all.

LAGARDE. Having a good leave?

JULIEN. Yes.

LAGARDE. M'm. . . . Good. . . . Do you know your lines yet, pussy dear?

COLOMBE. Yes, I think so, Monsieur Lagarde.

LAGARDE. Good. We're doing that scene this evening. Good. Yes.

He goes as he came.

JULIEN. Why did he call you his pussy?

COLOMBE. I don't know. It's just his way of being nice to me. He's helped me a lot with my part——

JULIEN. And why does he call you "dear"?

COLOMBE. Everyone calls each other dear in the theatre— I don't need to tell you that. He calls your mother dear.

DESFOURNETTES *bustles down the passage and gives a sprightly knock.*

DESFOURNETTES. Hullo-oh! Are you there, my little mousey?

JULIEN. Oh—a mouse now!

DESFOURNETTES. I was just going to tell you to be very careful tonight because your husband is . . . (*He opens the door and sees* JULIEN.) Oh! I beg your pardon.

JULIEN. Not at all.

DESFOURNETTES. Oh, but I do. . . . I was just coming to have a word with your wife. All going well?

JULIEN. Very well, thank you.

DESFOURNETTES. Yes—you're looking well, I must say.

JULIEN. Thank you. So everyone has told me.

DESFOURNETTES. M'm! I was just going to say . . . Good night.

He goes as he came.

JULIEN. My little mousey! . . . From that old wreck! It's revolting.

COLOMBE. You don't like it when I'm called a pussy, and you don't like it when I'm called a mousey—what do you want me to be called? Shall I insist on them all addressing me as Madame?

JULIEN. Why have you suddenly become so friendly with all these old fops?

COLOMBE. I'm not friendly with them. I see them every day. I work with them—that's all. You can't expect everyone to be as stand-offish as you. Besides, now and then I find the old sillies quite amusing.

JULIEN. *You* find *them* amusing?

Enter GEORGES.

GEORGES. Well—how are the moaning miseries? Glad to see one another?

JULIEN. Delighted.

GEORGES. You look it, I must say. . . . (*She takes*

68

COLOMBE'S *dress off a hanger and begins to dress her.*)
Some people don't know how lucky they are. There's
plenty of men who'd give a lot to be in your shoes and
have a little beauty like her to come back to. They're not
afraid to tell her so, either. Oh, she likes a compliment like
the rest of us, but she doesn't let it spoil her. All she thinks
of is her baby and her husband. You'd say these low necks
were made on purpose for her, wouldn't you? Got something worth showing off she has, too—just like two little
dumplings ready to go in the oven. Not like her ladyship:
it takes half an ironmonger's shop to keep hers in. . . .

> ROBINET *minces along the passage and flutters his
> knuckles on the door.*

Can I come ee-een? Are you there, my little wolfie?
JULIEN (*yelling*).   Yes—I'm here!
ROBINET (*bowled over at a masculine reply*). Oh, I'm sorry.
I'm sorry. I'm *so* sorry. I was only going to tell Made-
moiselle to be very careful because . . . No. No. It doesn't
matter. Or rather—yes! I know: it was that the King of
Spain is in front tonight. So do your best, little one—be
on your guard. And once again—so sorry. . . .

> *He goes as he came.*

JULIEN.   A wolf now! What are you—a menagerie? What
do you mean by letting that pot-bellied cad call you a
wolf? Didn't I forbid you to speak to him?
COLOMBE.   But he's the author of the play!
JULIEN.   There's no reason to speak to him! My little
pussy, my little mousey, my little wolfie! What next? And
why are they all telling you to be careful? Because they've
heard that *I'm* here?
COLOMBE.   I don't know what you're talking about. You're
being just a little tiresome.

69

JULIEN. And you—their little pet—lisping and purring through your painted lips—wipe it off! Wipe your lips when I tell you!

GEORGES. Master Julien—have some sense—you'll ruin her make-up!

JULIEN. Leave us alone!

GEORGES. You don't deserve her. She's too good for you—that's what she is——

JULIEN (*seizing her arm*). God damn you, woman, will you get out when I tell you!

GEORGES (*struggling*). That's right—knock us about! You're all the same! You don't understand us—no, not one of you!

JULIEN *slams the door behind her.* GEORGES *puts her ear instantly to the keyhole. She is joined by the* MANICURIST, *the* CHIROPODIST, SURETTE *in his stage costume, and all the other actors, gathering one by one in a silent eavesdropping audience at the door.* JULIEN *turns to* COLOMBE.

JULIEN. Now. . . . Who is he?

COLOMBE. Who, my darling?

JULIEN. Your lover.

COLOMBE. Julien, you're making things up. I haven't a lover.

JULIEN. It's no good lying. I have proof. You've been watched and you've been followed. Someone has written to me.

COLOMBE (*breaking away*). Who? Who has dared to write to you?

JULIEN. You see? Now you're frightened. I've a letter in my pocket which tells me everything—except his name. Now do you admit it?

COLOMBE. I want to know who has written to you.

70

JULIEN. That doesn't concern you.

COLOMBE. An anonymous letter, I suppose? I might have known it. And it's so much easier to believe the first piece of dirty gossip you hear than to have faith in your wife. The first spiteful little slut who can play on your jealousy and pride—she must be right and I telling lies— even if she daren't sign her name. . . . (*Her voice breaks with tears.*) Those two years when we were so happy— when I was loyal and loved you, and we lived on air with no money and no one to help me in the house—all that doesn't count any more. . . . Well, forget those days! Forget all the scraping and saving and making-do, and instead of giving me a kiss or a thank you believe all the worst you can hear! Oh, how miserable I am. . . . (*She falls crying bitterly on the settee.*)

JULIEN (*awkwardly*). I'm sorry, Colombe.

COLOMBE. Oh, it's easy enough to be sorry. It's done now. It's said. Now I know that you'll believe anyone—anyone rather than me.

JULIEN. I want to believe you.

COLOMBE. Was the letter signed?

JULIEN. Yes.

COLOMBE. Tell me her name! Just tell me her name, and I'll scratch her eyes out, the little cat!

JULIEN. It was a man who wrote to me.

COLOMBE (*after a rapid consideration*). I know who it was! Of course! Do you know that this precious tell-tale of yours was simply acting out of spite because he made some foul suggestions to me and I put him in his place?

JULIEN. Who has made foul suggestions to you? Tell me his name!

COLOMBE. You tell me who wrote to you first. Then I'll know if it's the same person. Just tell me the first letter of his name: it was a P, wasn't it?

71

JULIEN. No.

COLOMBE. Then . . . was it an R? That's who it was—an R—oh, the horrible beast!

JULIEN. It was neither a P nor an R.

COLOMBE. It wouldn't have been a W, would it? I'd believe him capable of anything if a woman turned him down. . . .

JULIEN. It was neither a P nor an R nor a W. So there are three men who might have written to me?

COLOMBE. Any man in the theatre might have done it. Any man who wanted to kiss me in a corner and was jealous if I said two words to someone else. You men are all the same. And don't look so innocent! You're not something apart.

JULIEN. Since I fell in love with you I have never looked at another woman. Never.

COLOMBE. What about those Boussac girls you spent so much time teaching to play waltzes on the piano?

JULIEN. They were only fifteen!

COLOMBE. Yes—and they were well advanced in other subjects besides music!

JULIEN. But—but—it's ridiculous!

COLOMBE. And the girl in the baker's shop?

JULIEN. What girl?

COLOMBE. You know perfectly well. You'd always grumble if I asked you to go shopping, but you were eager enough to slip round the corner for a loaf. That great fat blonde with a bust like a pair of balloons. . . . Oh, you're disgusting. I'm so miserable. I wish I was dead. . . .

She cries. JULIEN is embarrassed and helpless. In the passage there is a general opinion that the situation has now reversed itself for the better, and that the

moment has come to create a diversion. The HAIR-
DRESSER *is persuaded against his will to go in. He
knocks and enters.*

HAIRDRESSER. Madame Colombe, we're just going up.
Is there anything I can do for you?

JULIEN *pricks up his attention. He walks warily round the*
HAIRDRESSER, *who is attending to* COLOMBE'S *hair.*

COLOMBE (*smiling in the mirror*). Lucien, dear, you're an
angel. At least you make women look prettier for your
coming. Oh, I've been crying: just look what a sight I am.

HAIRDRESSER (*with rhythmic strokes of the comb*). Whatever you do, Madame Colombe, only makes you look
lovelier than ever. With you, work ceases to be a trouble
and becomes a pleasure.

COLOMBE (*smiling*). You're a gift from the gods, Lucien.
What would I do without you?

JULIEN. Look here, my man. . . .

HAIRDRESSER (*turning with his comb in the air*). Yes, sir?

JULIEN. You keep your attention for the top of her head.
That's where her hair is, isn't it?

HAIRDRESSER. Yes, sir. . . .

JULIEN. And do whatever you have to do with the comb—
not with your hands.

HAIRDRESSER. If you can instruct me, sir, how I can
dress Madame's bang with the comb alone——

JULIEN. Clear out! Go on—or I'll give you a bang you
won't forget! And a knock on the head that'll give you a
bloody shampoo!

HAIRDRESSER. Sir, I am an artist!

JULIEN. So am I. Birds of a feather. I'll see you in five
minutes and we'll have an artistic discussion!

He pushes him out and returns.

73

COLOMBE (*leaping up*). Ah—now I know who wrote to you! It was a Z.

JULIEN. No. It wasn't a Z.

COLOMBE. You're lying. I saw her. She was going out of the restaurant just as we came in. So all this fuss is simply because I went out to dinner with the hairdresser?

JULIEN (*staggered*). You—went out to dinner—with the hairdresser?

COLOMBE. Well, I have to eat, don't I? Do you want me to starve all the time you're away?

In the passage the HAIRDRESSER *is much mocked and very worried.*

JULIEN. Now I know enough! I'll thrash him till he screams!

He dashes to the door. The HAIRDRESSER *bursts through the crowd and trembles in the background.* COLOMBE *holds* JULIEN.

COLOMBE. Oh, darling, don't be so absurd! Do you think if I wanted to be unfaithful, I'd choose something like him? (*She laughs and kisses him.*) You great big booby! He grooms my hair with his hands because he knows his job—that's all! Do you think I'd let his hands touch another inch of me? I'd so much rather have yours. . . . (*She kisses them.*) And why, instead of making a rumpus all the time you've been back, why haven't you once taken me in your arms?

She snuggles up to him with her hands behind her back and offers him her lips.

JULIEN (*weakly*). But then—who is it? It would be so much better to tell me.

74

COLOMBE. No one! No one in the whole wide world! You're dreaming! Listen and I'll tell you a great secret. . . . It's you.

She kisses him. He relaxes and holds her. Great relief among the audience outside.

JULIEN. I love you so much. . . . If you have done anything foolish I'd forgive you, I promise. I'd try to forget . . . and go on just as before. I'm alone. . . . I couldn't live without you.

COLOMBE (*caressing him dreamily, all at once genuinely moved*). My poor little lost one. . . . So frightened of the world and everyone in it; and so much more alone than all the others. . . . But you're my dear, sweet, good-hearted own one. . . . And I'll never make you unhappy and I'll look after you always, for ever. . . .

JULIEN. But *why* did he call you his pussy?

COLOMBE. Who, my love? Lagarde?

Malicious joy among the audience. LAGARDE, *who finds all this is in very poor taste, is pushed to the fore.*

Oh, needless to say, he's paid his court like the others.

JULIEN. What has he suggested to you?

COLOMBE. Just to give me a little coaching in my part— along at his bachelor's den. "A drop of port, nibble a biscuit . . ." His room was supposed to be all oriental. That means that he has two old rugs with a pattern of palm trees and a hubble-bubble pipe that doesn't work— whenever you suck at the mouthpiece you swallow a gallon of dirty water!

JULIEN. But then. . . . You've been there?

COLOMBE (*a little put out*). No. At least—yes. But not alone. I went with Robinet to work on a scene.

JULIEN. So you do go out with them, you do go to their homes. . . .

75

COLOMBE. But I've told you—I only went with Robinet—he took me in a cab!

JULIEN. Were you alone with him in the cab?

COLOMBE. No—there was the driver! And I only took Robinet so that I shouldn't be alone with Lagarde. I could hardly take a third person so I wouldn't be alone with *him!*

JULIEN. I suppose you've forgotten the row I had with Robinet two years ago? He insulted you and I had to teach him a lesson.

COLOMBE. Well, now he's greatly improved, I promise you. Gallant, but polite.

ROBINET, *in great perturbation, has been pushed to the front row.*

JULIEN. Gallant, but polite! And you're all over him, I suppose, just to get yourself good parts. What do you exchange for your twenty extra lines? Let him kiss your wrist instead of your hand? Let him take your arm in a dark carriage and give him every time another inch more? And what does it matter if he's old, if he's bald and disgusting, if the bubbles of spit that he sprays when he talks are always dripping from his dyed moustache? Well, he won't get away with it this time! This time I'll teach him a lesson he'll never forget!

He is trying to get out, and on the other side of the door ROBINET *is trying to run away.* COLOMBE *is holding on to* JULIEN *and laughing like a maniac.*

COLOMBE. Darling, oh my darling, darling—don't be so silly! Oh—it's too funny—too funny for words!

JULIEN. What's funny? That I'm hurt and upset?

COLOMBE (*as best she can through peals of laughter*). N-no! His . . . his . . . the bubbles of spit that he s-sprays when

76

he talks! It's just what he does! And when he's close to you the bubbles burst—and wet you all over your nose! My darling—can you see me in the arms of that—that syringe? Can you see him—making his flowery speeches—standing in nothing but his—his *drawers?*

She is hysterical with giggling. Little by little JULIEN *is won over.*

JULIEN. I must say . . . I really must say . . . Robinet in his drawers—would be quite a sight!

COLOMBE (*in a shriek of helpless laughter*). And do you know—his drawers—they're sky blue—with pink lace!

She suddenly stops dead. JULIEN *too.*

JULIEN. How do you know?

COLOMBE. But darling, everybody knows it.

JULIEN. Who has told you?

COLOMBE (*an inspiration*). Desfournettes.

JULIEN. Desfournettes? You have that sort of conversation with Desfournettes? Conversation about the author's underwear?

COLOMBE. Now listen, darling, and I'll tell you. . . .

JULIEN. You haven't been up to his office, have you?

COLOMBE. No! Or rather—yes—once. Listen! You won't let me explain. It was when I went up to sign my contract. (*She makes up her mind.*) Yes. I'll tell you the truth. He tried . . . Yes, he tried like all the others. I slapped his face. And because he thought that I must prefer someone else—Robinet perhaps—just out of jealousy he told me about Robinet's underwear. That's all. You see, my darling, I've told you the truth.

JULIEN (*striking her suddenly across the face*). You whore! You grubby little whore like all the rest! My God, I'll take that self-satisfied grin off his face for good and all!

COLOMBE *gives a shriek and falls in a faint.* JULIEN
rushes to the door. MADAME ALEXANDRA *in full
costume brushes through the crowd and confronts*
JULIEN. GEORGES *slips in to attend to* COLOMBE.

JULIEN. Get out of my way! I want Desfournettes!

MME. ALEXANDRA. Why must the whole theatre be
thrown into an uproar whenever you appear? Can't you
open your stupid mouth without shouting and making a
scene?

JULIEN. It's all your fault! Yours! You defiled her! You
all defiled her!

MME. ALEXANDRA. Silence! I am your mother!

JULIEN (*suddenly quiet*). My mother. . . . Yes, you are my
mother. . . .Unhappily you are.

MME. ALEXANDRA. Do you think it's any happier for
me? Always giving out money, endless fuss, ridiculous
scenes—just as it was with your father! Go away and
leave this child in peace. She's having some amusement
now, seeing life. What do you and your father's kind
imagine a woman's life is? An eternal worship of creatures
like you, just because you've had the good taste to choose
us? Women, my little boy, only belong to a man for so
long as he makes it worth while. . . . (*In a shriek at*
SURETTE.) Well, call them on-stage!

SURETTE. But the girl's fainted, Madame!

GEORGES. You can't expect her to go on and give a
performance. . . .

MME. ALEXANDRA. In this theatre I do not expect anyone
to give a performance! *I* give the performance! Get her
down!

*She goes. Everyone presses back to let her pass, while
the bell rings and* SURETTE *calls:*

SURETTE. On stage, for Act *One*, please! On stage for Act *One*, please!

> *At these words* COLOMBE *recovers with astonishing rapidity. She hurries to the glass.*

COLOMBE. Do I look too dreadful?

GEORGES. No—you'll do. Come along quick—I'll give you a tidy downstairs.

> *Everyone has gone. All the dressing-room doors are open.* JULIEN *is alone. Down below we hear the orchestra playing the overture.* PAUL *appears. He walks gaily down the passage in time to the music carrying a bouquet of flowers. He wheels into* COLOMBE'S *room and stops suddenly, staggered to see* JULIEN. *He stands awkwardly, not knowing what to do with his embarrassing bouquet.*

JULIEN. So . . . it's you.

PAUL. Yes. It's me. Have you got leave?

JULIEN. I should have guessed it was you.

PAUL. Aren't you pleased to see me? I brought your wife some flowers. You're looking very well.

JULIEN. Yes. I'm looking very well.

PAUL. Enjoying your new life?

JULIEN. No.

PAUL (*trying to keep up his banter*). A bit hard on the feet, isn't it? They say it's a good idea to soap your socks.

> *He tries to laugh, but is stopped by* JULIEN'S *expression.*

JULIEN. Do you want to laugh about it?

PAUL. No.

> *A silence.*

JULIEN. You. . . . Why you?

PAUL (*gently, after a pause*). You were away. We were together. She's young, pretty. . . . You know how it is.

JULIEN. No, I don't know how it is. I shall never know.

PAUL. I suppose not. . . . You're a better person than I am. You always have been. You've always been grown up and able to resist yourself. I've never learned anything, except how to trail after women in the wings of a theatre. First, mother . . . then others. . . . And so it's gone on. I'm no good, Julien. But at least I know it.

JULIEN. Yes.

PAUL. Well, what do you want to do?

> JULIEN *doesn't move.*

You ought to have given me a hiding more often when we were boys. You'd have done me good. Well, you can hit me now. I'm waiting.

JULIEN. No. I don't want to hit you. All I want is to understand.

PAUL. Won't you teach me my lesson? That's what I expected. I took the risk. I had that much courage.

JULIEN. Look at me.

PAUL. I can't.

JULIEN. Look at me.

PAUL. Hit me if you like. But don't ask me to look at you.

JULIEN (*lifting his head roughly*). Yes—you'll look at me. (*He searches in his face.*) You're not even good-looking. A straight nose. But why should one fraction of bone and gristle make so much difference? A wet little mouth, and lips like a girl's. . . . The eyes of a drunkard, and the traces of your furtive little joys in every pore. . . . Twenty-one. . . . A cynical old lecher at twenty-one.

PAUL. You needn't think I'm proud of myself. . . . Oh, how can I explain, when you don't know anything about life?

80

JULIEN. I'm beginning to learn.

PAUL (*with an attempt at ease*). Why don't you go back to the army and forget all about us? I'm sure you're far better at handling a gun than a woman!

JULIEN (*still holding him*). Keep your second-hand cynical jokes to pass round your friends in the bars. In all your life nothing has ever moved you. Has it?

PAUL. I have feelings like everyone else. But——

JULIEN. But you pay no attention. They get in the way of your amusements. . . . Oh, if only you were at least elegant. . . . If only I could think that you dazzled her and turned her head. But you dress like a bookmaker's clerk with your loud ties and your flashy rings. . . . Why? Why should it be you?

PAUL. Do you think I know the answer? Go and ask her!

JULIEN. I want to know. I want to know why. Kiss me, as you did her.

PAUL. Have you gone mad? Let me go!

JULIEN. Kiss me. Kiss me as you did her. Show me why.

PAUL. Let go—you'll choke me——

JULIEN. Kiss me, kiss me, you little sofa seducer! Show me what makes them love you—show me what makes them weak!

PAUL. No! No!

> JULIEN *forces their mouths together; then, revolted, flings him roughly away. He wipes his mouth with the back of his hand.*

JULIEN. I don't understand.

CURTAIN

ACT THREE

*The stage of the theatre during an evening performance. We
are looking towards the proscenium from the back of the
stage setting. What appears to the audience as a Venetian
courtyard is, from here, a perspective of the reverse sides
of the flats and ground-rows. A wire hangs down behind
the last ground-row supporting a cardboard moon which
is about to be raised by a stage hand in the wings. A
gondola waits just off stage. The gondolier is reading a
newspaper, and some stage hands on the opposite side
are ready to pull him across with a rope.* MADAME
ALEXANDRA *and* LAGARDE *are in full flood.*
COLOMBE *stands aside in the part of a confidante.*

MME. ALEXANDRA.
　　O too long have I loved in sighs and dreams,
　　And never known the touch that now, it seems,
　　Sends hastening messengers thro' every vein,
　　With tidings part of pleasure, part sweet pain.
LAGARDE.
　　My love, is't you?
MME. ALEXANDRA.
　　　　　　　　Is't me? I only know
　　A girl stood here before, so long ago
　　And yet, an instant hence; now woman stands,
　　Possessed of new-found wisdom.
　　　　　　　　　　Your commands
　　Are laws to me, your slightest change
　　Of face, of mood, of whim—however strange—
　　Are Emperors to my enslaved will. . . .
　　O tongue, be modest! Urgent heart be still!

LAGARDE.

    Fear not your ardour! Passion long confined
    Bursts like a broken sluice to flood the mind,
    And brings forth e'en in deserts, unknown flowers. . . .

MME. ALEXANDRA.

    O, how my fancy scales the topmost towers,
    Peaks, pinnacles and Paradise of bliss!
    Have I his heart? And can my heart be his?

LAGARDE.

    The rising moon is witness to our vows!

COLOMBE.

    Hush! See—who's this who comes?

MME. ALEXANDRA.

                It is my spouse!

LAGARDE.

    We are discovered!

MME. ALEXANDRA.

             No! Rise not! Proclaim,
    This love of ours is proud, and feels no shame!

    SURETTE *enters. He is very grandly dressed as a Venetian nobleman.*

SURETTE.

    What's this? What's this? Rudolpho and my wife?

MME. ALEXANDRA.

    I love this man!

SURETTE.

            Such love might cost a life.

    LAGARDE *draws his sword.*

LAGARDE.

    'Twill be sold dear! Come, words have had their say!

    SURETTE *raises his hand in a gesture of infinite nobility.*

SURETTE.

> Young hothead, sheath your steel. But yesterday
> I would have fought with you. One life is spared,
> Yet thousands will be lost. War is declared!

LAGARDE.　　War?

MME. ALEXANDRA.　　War?

SURETTE.

> 　　　　Ay, war. Since dawn a mighty force
> Invades our sacred soil.

LAGARDE.

> 　　　My horse! My horse!

A trumpet call in the distance. MADAME ALEXANDRA
weeps loudly. LAGARDE *unbuckles his rapier.*

> Bring me my two-edged sword! Sound the alarm!
> Such toys as this do insufficient harm
> To those who dare our frontiers desecrate!
> My country calls! Thank God you weren't too late!

*A servant brings him a sword. Fanfares. Figures rush to
and fro with lighted torches.*

SURETTE.

> Thus in his country's need your lover hears
> A nobler call than thine, for all these tears . . .

*He wipes away a tear of his own, pulls himself together
and draws his sword with a splendid gesture.*

> Young man, let's march, and in the clash of war
> Forget that wives scarce wed may play the whore!

LAGARDE.

> Farewell, forgive, forget—all lover's woes
> Must now give place to combat 'gainst our foes!

LAGARDE *and* SURETTE *make a tremendous exit to
the sound of trumpets, marching feet, cheers and bells.*

MADAME ALEXANDRA *falls weeping into the arms*
of COLOMBE.

COLOMBE.

O weep not so! Your true love will return,
And love's warm embers once again will burn.

MME. ALEXANDRA.

He may return. But will my heart be true?

COLOMBE.

"Why, surely so. . . ."

MME. ALEXANDRA.

Am I not twenty-two?
And passion's cup does not improve, like wine,
By being kept untasted. Sister mine,
Would it be cruel to dance? I hear the strings,
That cunning fingers thrill with whisperings.
Across the water sounds the serenade:
Shall we thus mourn, and let our beauty fade
In loveless chastity?

COLOMBE.

The gondolier
Awaits your pleasure.

MME. ALEXANDRA.

Bid him gently steer
Unto some place where wounded lovers may
Forget their woes, in mirth and pleasures gay.

COLOMBE.

My mistress bids you smoothly to transport
This fragile burden to the Doge's Court
Where pleasure reigns supreme.

MME. ALEXANDRA.

The moon is high,
And looks, methinks, with mute consent as I
Prepare to celebrate, the Fates obeyed,
Love lost, Love found again—in Masquerade!

*As the gondola is tugged across the stage, the scene fills
with masked couples who dance on from the wings.*
MADAME ALEXANDRA *waves to them as she goes.
To the music of the finale, the curtain falls. Tremendous
applause. Repeated curtains: the company,* MADAME
ALEXANDRA *and* LAGARDE, MADAME ALEXANDRA
alone.

LAGARDE (*taking off his wig as he goes*).   Phew! What a
damn silly lot of swine out there tonight!

As MADAME ALEXANDRA *takes a call alone,* JULIEN
*appears in the wings. As the curtain falls, he runs on
to the stage.*

JULIEN.   Colombe!

DESFOURNETTES *and* ROBINET *and the stage hands
rush on from the wings to chase him off.*

MME. ALEXANDRA.   Who let that lunatic on the stage?
SURETTE.   Madame! Another curtain! They're calling for
you!
MME. ALEXANDRA.   Desfournettes, the reception is
ruined! Who let him come in? It's an insult! So long as
I live I'll never play for you again!

*She storms off, followed by her retinue. The lights go
out and the scenery is hoisted to the flies. There is
nothing left but the bare stage in the light of a single
lamp, and the gondola that stands between* JULIEN *and*
COLOMBE.

JULIEN.   Colombe. All this time I've walked about the
streets. I must talk to you.
COLOMBE.   I must go and change.
JULIEN.   No. I want to talk to you here. I can't bear to go
upstairs among the others.

COLOMBE. Well, talk, then. I'm listening.

JULIEN. I've spoken to Paul.

COLOMBE. Yes.

JULIEN. He's told me everything. Have you seen him since?

COLOMBE. Yes.

JULIEN. You can imagine what it was like; especially for me.

COLOMBE. I'm sorry if I've made you unhappy.

JULIEN. Thinking it over, I realise how much I've been to blame. I left you alone together. You were both young and thoughtless. And perhaps I bored you sometimes by preaching to you, and trying to make you what I wanted you to be.

COLOMBE. Yes.

JULIEN. So I've decided to forgive you. All I ask is that you should help me to understand.

COLOMBE (*who has listened very patiently*). It would take a very long time to explain it to you. And I mustn't be late. Shall we go up to the dressing-room?

JULIEN. What mustn't you be late for?

COLOMBE. This supper party I told you about.

JULIEN. You aren't seriously thinking of going to a supper party after all that's happened? My leave finishes tomorrow. . . .

COLOMBE. I've told you that it's a very important engagement.

JULIEN. You can just—put everything out of mind—and go and amuse yourself with other people?

COLOMBE. If you think I get any amusement out of going to Maxim's, you're mistaken. I have to think of my future, that's all.

JULIEN. Colombe—I'm not dreaming, am I? You never used to be like this. When we had a quarrel, you were always the first to make it up. . . .

COLOMBE. That's all I want now, my darling. I don't want to quarrel with you—I want you to be happy. All I ask is that you should be sensible, and not make me late for my party.

JULIEN. It can't be true! You can't have stopped loving me so suddenly. . . .

START

COLOMBE. Who said I'd stopped loving you?

JULIEN. Colombe, you may have done something foolish, but you're still my wife. We've our future to think of—all the things we've planned and hoped for—the future of our child!

COLOMBE. Oh, yes! I might have known you'd bring up the child! What's his future got to do with yours?

JULIEN. Everything!

COLOMBE. Who's looked after him since the day he was born? Who bought the cradle he's sleeping in now? Who'll wake him up in the morning and wash him and give him his breakfast? You . . . ? He's my son, and I love him, and I'll always make sure he has everything he needs. What does he care for our little squabbles? When he gets bigger I shall tell him that you made me unhappy, and that I was so fed up with you that one day I couldn't stand it any longer.

JULIEN. So I've made you unhappy?

COLOMBE. Yes.

JULIEN. I've given you everything—

COLOMBE. Oh, no! Not everything. Everything you could spare, everything you wanted to give. That's not enough. You liked to sit at home in the evenings—so we never went out. "What fun it is," you'd say, "to sit snugly side by side in our little room with no one else to have to talk to." And I was so young, I knew so little, my head was so stuffed with your sacred opinions of right and wrong, that I couldn't do anything but say "Yes". But I would rather have gone out and danced.

JULIEN. ~~But we used to go to dances. . . .~~

COLOMBE. ~~Twice, in two years. And you trod on my toes. And when other men asked me to dance you wouldn't let me.~~

JULIEN. ~~But—you loved me—it was only natural . . .~~

COLOMBE. Yes, I loved you. But I loved dancing, too. And instead of listening to you tearing the universe to shreds, I would rather have slipped into the arms of the first fool who could waltz me round the floor and make me laugh. You see, I'm only quite a simple, stupid person; not a superior being like you. And it's the simple, stupid people I prefer to go about with; at least they live, and at least they're amusing.

JULIEN. ~~But didn't we live too? Didn't we have our amusements?~~

COLOMBE. ~~Yes—Mozart and Beethoven!~~

JULIEN. ~~But you used to like to hear me play!~~

COLOMBE. ~~I had to pretend to like it. The music I loved was the waltzes and polkas they played in the café across the street. But you didn't like to hear it, and you closed the windows.~~

JULIEN. ~~I wanted to train you to appreciate beauty. . . .~~

COLOMBE. Who are you to tell me what's beautiful and what isn't? Whatever one loves is beautiful: and I love bouquets of flowers, and dressing up, and dancing. . . .

JULIEN. ~~But we hadn't any money~~ *YOU SAID WE HADN'T ANY MONEY.*

COLOMBE. Only because it was beneath your dignity to make any. Your art must always come before everything—your future as a great pianist. And so that you could become a great pianist on a platform, I had to become an unpaid drudge in the kitchen, and be sworn at if I knocked two pots together and made a noise that disturbed your studies. And if I'd gone on with it, and if one day you'd ever become a great pianist, a fine sight I would have been at the grand reception in your honour, with my red hands and my broken nails! Or perhaps, just for *that* occasion, you'd have bought me a pair of gloves to hide them in? My first pair of gloves in two years. . . .

JULIEN. How can you say such things?

COLOMBE. I can say them because now it's all over. Now, I can live for myself. I only began to be happy the day after you'd gone. I woke up, the sun was shining, I drew back the curtains and for the first time there was nothing but happiness in the street. The baker's boy whistled when he saw me at the window, and I smiled and said "Good morning", and there was no one to blame me all the rest of the day because I'd answered him. And if the postman rang the bell before I was up, there was no one to tell me I was a fallen woman if I opened the door in my night-dress. He was a happier postman for seeing a pretty girl in her nightie, and I was a happier girl in seeing that it gave him pleasure. I cleaned the rooms as if it were a game, and I put a basin of water in the sunshine and stood in it naked, to wash myself—and what did it matter if the old man opposite was getting a treat through his binoculars? It was a natural joy to both of us, a present from God as much as the sun on the trees.

JULIEN. But I was only jealous because I loved you! If . . . any other man loves you, he'll be just the same.

COLOMBE. If he is jealous, at least he'll be gay and make me laugh.

JULIEN. Paul doesn't love you—you know that. . . .

COLOMBE. He loves me in the way that I want to be loved. He makes me happy, he tells me I'm pretty, he brings me little presents, he senses what I want. . . .

JULIEN. I, I, I! You think of nothing but yourself!

COLOMBE.   Yes. It's a word that I've only just learned. . . . And now if I don't go I shall be late. There's nothing more to be said.

JULIEN.   No! (*He takes her by the wrist.*)

COLOMBE.   Let me go!

JULIEN.   No!

COLOMBE.   You're hurting me! Yes—go on! Show you're the strongest! Hurt me and hit me—you've done it before! Do you think I've forgotten the last time? I'll never forget.

JOSEPH *and* LEON *come on from the wings.*

LEON.   Excuse me, sir, but we've got to strike the gondola. D'you mind?

JULIEN *steps aside and the gondola is taken away. He draws* COLOMBE *to him and they stand face to face.*

JULIEN.   I want to ask you just one thing. Will you promise to give me an answer?

COLOMBE.   I don't know. Ask what you want.

JULIEN.   When you saw me in your dressing-room, why did you run to me and put your arms round my neck?

COLOMBE.   Because I was pleased to see you. That's the truth.

JULIEN.   Why did you seem to care so much about how I was getting on?

COLOMBE.   Because I didn't like to think you were unhappy.

JULIEN.   And when I told you my suspicions and questioned you, why did you deny everything and swear that you loved me?

COLOMBE.   Because I do love you; because you're going away tomorrow and I didn't want you to be miserable, far away and all by yourself.

JULIEN.   Why did you take my hands and kiss them and put my arms around you?

COLOMBE.   So that you should believe me; and to please you.

JULIEN.   And if I had believed you, and if I hadn't got the truth out of Paul, would you have come back tonight and slept with me?

COLOMBE.   Yes.

JULIEN.   You would have let me love you?

COLOMBE.   Yes.

JULIEN (*after a pause*).   I don't understand.

COLOMBE.   You'll never understand anything that matters. You didn't understand when I was unhappy at home; you don't understand why I'm so miserable now. And everyone will know that I've been crying.

JULIEN.   My poor little Colombe. All you can think of is your smart friends waiting for you at supper. . . . I loved you once with so many kinds of love. . . . I was ready to forget all the liberty I'd known, the seas I'd never crossed, and the sights I'd never seen . . . and the girls I used to joke with on the corners of the streets—I passed them by without a glance and left them to my old friends who were free. . . . All this I gave up without regret, just to become a dull commonplace old husband, begging the money for his tobacco and grumbling if he couldn't read the newspaper in peace. . . . That seemed to me—then—enough adventure for the whole span of my life; because I loved you. . . .

A silence.

COLOMBE.   Well, now you can go round the world if you want to. You can pick up the girls you see in the streets. You can try asking them to give up everything for you—as you did me two years ago.

JULIEN. Yes. I could.

COLOMBE. And just as you did me, you'll take them in with your soulful airs, your wonderful mind, and your poor bruised heart. Oh, what a fool I was, what a fool . . .!

JULIEN. Colombe!

COLOMBE. Colombe. . . . Such a little innocent you thought her, didn't you? The little flower girl who gave old gentlemen a thrill by pinning carnations in their buttonholes. . . .

JULIEN. No! You were just as I thought you! That *was* Colombe. You are . . . someone else.

He studies her face as though for the last time.

There's one thing I'm afraid of, more than anything else. That one day you'll sink so low that I'll have no love left for you. That you'll be all alone in the world, with your poor little body offered to the first comer; your little face set hard with secrets you can tell to no one; all alone, with no one to love you, and no one to love except yourself.

COLOMBE (*quite casually*). You're hurting me. My arms won't be fit to be seen.

JULIEN. Very well. . . . You'll be late. . . . Go and get dressed for your party.

She moves away without a glance.

Colombe!

COLOMBE. Yes?

JULIEN. If while you're dressing you think you'd rather not go—I'll be waiting for you here. Here, on this stage, where we first met, two years ago. . . .

She shrugs her shoulders and goes. Enter SURETTE.

SURETTE. Bitches, the whole lot of 'em, eh? You give them everything, you work like a black to support them, they roll on their backs and lick your hands—and then one fine day some cocky little pup gives them the wink and they're off without even a thank you. I've been married, too, you know. My mother found me a fat young sow from the country. There were two of them—sisters—and I chose the uglier, thinking she'd be easier to keep. It won't be any different in the dark, I thought, and the uglier they are, the better they work about the house. She was stupid as they make 'em, with a wall eye into the bargain, but guaranteed intacta and sound in wind and limb. I thought I was on clover. I went off on a fortnight's tour, got back a day earlier than she expected, and what do you think I found in my bed? An undertaker! He lived above us and had a hare lip and was worse to look at than she was. Not a stitch on—neither of 'em. A fine sight that was.

JULIEN. Get out! Go away! Leave me alone.

SURETTE. But at times like this you mustn't be left to yourself. Why don't we slip out and have a chat over a glass of beer?

JULIEN. I'm waiting for Colombe.

SURETTE. If you're waiting for the little flower girl you married, you'll wait all your life, my friend. She doesn't exist any more—outside your imagination.

JULIEN. Get out, will you, or I'll knock you down!

SURETTE. Very well, very well—I'm going. . . . (*At a safe distance*.) But that's hardly the way to speak—to a colleague.

> *He goes, tittering. Enter* MADAME ALEXANDRA, *followed by* GEORGES. *She is wrapped in rugs and shawls and walks with the aid of a stick.*

JULIEN (*running to her*). Mother!

MME. ALEXANDRA. What do you mean—mother? Have you gone mad?

JULIEN. Oh, mother, I'm so unhappy!

MME. ALEXANDRA. You have sown, my son, now you must reap.

JULIEN. I loved her. I still love her. I'll always love her.

MME. ALEXANDRA. Yes. . . . Your father would always have loved me. That was what frightened me. Why must you always think that love is for eternity? What do you mean when you say "for life"? Our clothes change with the fashions; we move from one house to another; fruit goes rotten; flowers fade. . . . A doctor will tell you that after seven years there isn't a single cell in your body that hasn't changed. We change and decompose from the day we are born, and yet you still go on hoping that love will stay fresh and uncorrupted. Where did you learn to believe such things, you and your father? At school, or in trashy novels? Your heads are so full of second-hand romance that you've forgotten to learn how to live. If your father had started life as I did at thirteen in the Folies Bergères, he would have known better than to kill himself for love. . . . Come along, Georges. Have you got my medicine? And my spectacles? And my script? I've two hundred lines of Corneille to learn for the morning.

JULIEN. Mother—you must have been unhappy too! Won't you talk to me? Tonight I'm so much alone.

MME. ALEXANDRA. You will always be alone—just like your father.

JULIEN. But I love her!

MME. ALEXANDRA. Good. That is a fact. Another fact of equal importance is that she doesn't love you. Well, what do you want her to do about it? Pretend to love you all her life, just because you love her? Drive herself mad for fifty years because you think it might help you? Go to bed, and tomorrow go back and play soldiers. (*She turns.*) Was it . . . money you wanted to ask me for?

95

JULIEN. No thank you, Mother. Not money.

MME. ALEXANDRA. Well. . . . Good luck. If you don't want to end up like your father, try to get on without asking life to give you quite so much. And forget about "love eternal".

> *She goes, followed by* GEORGES. JULIEN *goes to a piano in the wings. He plays a few random notes. They echo in the air. He hears nothing, his head falls on the keyboard. The lights dim. In the darkness a distant piano plays a waltz. It grows louder and louder until it might be being played on the stage. The light returns, and* JULIEN, *in his civilian clothes, is playing the waltz on the same piano. The stage is still empty and lit by the working light, but rays of sunshine blaze down from the flies.* COLOMBE *enters carrying a great bouquet of flowers. She seems timid and lost. She sees* JULIEN *and comes to him.*

COLOMBE. Excuse me, sir. Can you tell me the way to Madame Alexandra's dressing-room?

JULIEN (*still playing*). It's on the first floor. You can wait for her here if you like—she'll be coming down to rehearse. I'm waiting for her, too. You'll save yourself a flight of stairs and an imperial row—she's busy smashing the furniture.

COLOMBE. Has something gone wrong?

JULIEN. In the theatre something has always gone wrong.

COLOMBE. She's such a wonderful actress! I can't get over it that I may meet her face to face.

JULIEN. When you see her face, I doubt if you'll get over that either.

COLOMBE. That's not a very nice thing to say. . . . How old is she?

JULIEN. Tomorrow is her hundredth birthday.

COLOMBE. Don't be so silly. I've seen her on the stage. Once I was given some seats.

JULIEN. Oh, on the stage it's a different matter. She looks fully eighty years younger.

COLOMBE. You ought to be ashamed of yourself. What would she say if she heard you?

JULIEN. She's quite used to it. She's my mother.

He is still playing.

COLOMBE. What?

JULIEN. Oh, don't think I'm proud of it. . . . What's your name?

COLOMBE. Colombe.

JULIEN. Colombe. . . . Mine's Julien.

A sudden little silence.

Is it fun to work for a florist?

COLOMBE. Not always as much fun—as today.

JULIEN. You must see plenty of life.

COLOMBE. Yes. . . . But then it's always old gentlemen who buy flowers.

JULIEN. I can't help being glad.

COLOMBE. Why?

JULIEN. Never mind why. When I'm rich I'll come and buy your flowers—and present them back to you.

COLOMBE. Will you?

JULIEN. I promise. Does anyone ever give you flowers?

COLOMBE. No.

JULIEN. Not even your young man?

COLOMBE. I haven't one.

JULIEN. Then I must be the first.

He breaks a rose from the bouquet.

COLOMBE. Oh—the bouquet! You've spoiled it! You'll get me into dreadful trouble——

JULIEN. Don't worry—I'll take the blame. There'll be trouble anyway when she finds me here.

COLOMBE (*smelling the rose*). It's funny . . . when flowers are given to you they seem quite different. . . . Doesn't your mother like you coming to the theatre?

JULIEN. Not very much.

COLOMBE. I suppose she thinks you'll fall into bad company.

JULIEN (*laughing*). Oh, you're wonderful. . . . No. She's always afraid that I've come to ask her for money.

Their conversation runs dry.

And—do you earn a lot of money working in a flower shop?

COLOMBE. Oh, with tips I make about a hundred francs a month.

JULIEN. Suppose I came along to the shop one night to take you out to supper. . . . You wouldn't insist on going to Maxim's?

COLOMBE. I don't even know where it is. But I once went to Poccardi's.

JULIEN. Then I'll take you back to Poccardi's. . . . What does the money matter? We'll send the bill to the old girl.

COLOMBE. When shall we go?

JULIEN. This evening? Why wait?

COLOMBE. But we might miss one another. This is my last errand, and I'm not going back to the shop.

JULIEN (*taking her hand*). Then let's go now.

COLOMBE. But what about the bouquet?

JULIEN. Leave it. It's large enough—they can hardly miss it.

COLOMBE. But I must wait for my tip.

JULIEN. Of course! If we're going to Poccardi's you'll have to pay for the tram.

COLOMBE. You know. . . . I don't always say "Yes" like this straight out at once. Usually I say "No". This is the first time.

JULIEN. I don't usually make such an offer. It's the first time for me too. But . . . I ought to warn you before you come to Poccardi's. . . . I'm not a very nice sort of person. I've got a bad reputation. I don't like people, and they don't like me.

COLOMBE. I don't believe it.

JULIEN. It's true. It's because I'm not kind and gentle. Somehow, I can't be.

COLOMBE. But I think you're very kind.

JULIEN. With you—yes. Though I don't know why. Have you ever been to the Zoo?

COLOMBE. Yes.

JULIEN. Do you ever stand in front of the cage full of bears? Do you like to watch them, mauling with their clumsy paws? Do you think you'd have the patience to tame one?

COLOMBE (*close beside him*). Yes. . . .

JULIEN. Oh, if only this could come true, as it does in stories! True all at once, and for always! Promise that you'll stay faithful to me until this evening? Just until we get to Poccardi's?

COLOMBE. I promise.

JULIEN. Cross your heart.

COLOMBE. I cross my heart.

JULIEN. Kiss me. Is it too soon?

COLOMBE. No . . .

Enter MADAME ALEXANDRA *followed by her staff*, ROBINET, DESFOURNETTES, SURETTE, *etc.*

99

MME. ALEXANDRA. Drabs! Muck! Trollops from the gutter! Where did you find them? Each is worse than the other and we open in three days! (*She sees* JULIEN.) As if I hadn't enough on my hands without you. What are you doing here?

JULIEN. Darling Mumsy—I am kissing a flower girl.

MME. ALEXANDRA. Nonsense! You've only come to ask me for money. Desfournettes: find me ten more girls to audition this evening.

DESFOURNETTES. But the little dark one you saw this afternoon. . . .

MME. ALEXANDRA. Your little dark one was a scarecrow. . . .

DESFOURNETTES. Oh, come now—she only has to sing a song and speak two lines. . . .

ROBINET. But, my dears, we're all out of our minds! What are we looking for?

DESFOURNETTES. A little flower girl for the last act.

ROBINET. Exactly! A little flower girl who will really look like a flower girl. Then just look here! The real thing—and a ravishing beauty as well!

MME. ALEXANDRA. H'm. . . . Turn around, girl. Let's see your legs.

COLOMBE. My legs?

MME. ALEXANDRA. Yes—you know where they are, don't you?

ROBINET. Now you've frightened the poor little thing. Come along now, show us your legs. (*He lifts her skirts.*)

COLOMBE (*clutching her skirts*). Oh—sir!

ROBINET. Don't worry—just a little higher.

DESFOURNETTES. Our interest is purely æsthetic.

MME. ALEXANDRA. Have you ever done any singing, child?

COLOMBE. Only to myself.

ROBINET. "Only to myself!" Exquisite!

MME. ALEXANDRA. Do you know some little song you could try for us?

COLOMBE. I don't know, Madame.

MME. ALEXANDRA. Surely you know *Lovers' Regrets*, don't you? That's what the girl sings in the play.

COLOMBE. Oh yes—I think I know that.

MME. ALEXANDRA. We'll see. And if you can sing it in tune we'll give you five francs a performance.

DESFOURNETTES. Four.

MME. ALEXANDRA. Four. Julien! Where is that oaf? He's never here when he's wanted.

JULIEN (*in a corner*). I'm here.

MME. ALEXANDRA. Accompany the child on the piano.

JULIEN. No.

MME. ALEXANDRA. Why not?

JULIEN. I've a bad finger.

MME. ALEXANDRA. Nonsense! You just don't want to.

PAUL *has just entered.*

Paul! Paul, dear boy, could you play us *Lovers' Regrets* with one finger on the piano?

PAUL. My dear Mumsy, I can play Wagner with one finger.

MME. ALEXANDRA. Then do us a favour and accompany this child we're auditioning. Don't be nervous, little one, all we're concerned with is to get this thing settled and go and have dinner.

PAUL (*at the piano*). Are you ready?

COLOMBE *sings, at first stifled with nerves, but eventually very prettily:*

101

COLOMBE.

> "You and I were lonely,
> We'd kiss and we'd sigh;
> We thought if we married
> Our love couldn't die.
> Why did we swear that we'd always be true. . . ."

As she sings ROBINET *has been fondling her and lifting her skirts.*

JULIEN. That's enough!

ROBINET. I'm not doing any harm——

JULIEN. I said that's enough—leave her alone!

ROBINET. But we must see her legs—we're using them in the play.

JULIEN. All right, you've asked for it! Take that!

He kicks ROBINET *under the coat tails. Pandemonium.*

DESFOURNETTES. Joseph! Leon!

MME. ALEXANDRA. Is this a theatre or a madhouse?

ROBINET. The great big bully—he's torn my trousers!

MME. ALEXANDRA. Girl, that's enough. You're engaged.

JULIEN (*held by the stage hands*). Poccardi's! Remember— you promised!

MME. ALEXANDRA. Throw him out!

COLOMBE. Let him go! Let him go! (*She runs to* JULIEN.) I hate you all! I want to go to Poccardi's!

MME. ALEXANDRA. But don't you understand? You're engaged. You're rehearsing this evening.

COLOMBE. I've another engagement—and one that I'm going to keep.

PAUL. She's in love!

MME. ALEXANDRA. I've been in love twenty-two times. That's never stopped me signing a contract.

She sweeps out, followed by her retinue.

102

ROBINET (*as he goes*).   Nasty, conceited little squirt!

He saves himself as quickly as dignity will permit, aided by COLOMBE, *who is restraining* JULIEN. *The three of them are left alone.*

COLOMBE.   Let him go.

JULIEN.   Did you hear what he said to me?

COLOMBE.   No. I was thinking of something else: of how happy I am.

PAUL (*who is still sitting at the piano*).   How long have you two known one another?

JULIEN.   Just about an hour.

COLOMBE.   Don't tell him. He won't believe us.

PAUL.   And you'd rather spend an evening with this old bear at Poccardi's than get a chance of going on the stage? One meets such a girl only once in a thousand years. Where did you find her?

JULIEN.   In my heart.

PAUL.   I rather doubt that. . . . You won't make her too unhappy, will you? You won't preach at her too much?

JULIEN (*with a grin*).   No.

PAUL.   Best wishes, then. . . . Oh, incidentally, I stung Mamma for quite a bit yesterday . . . shall we split the booty?

JULIEN.   That's very decent of you.

PAUL.   No—pure selfishness. It means I can share a little in your party at Poccardi's. (*He hands the money.*) Have a good time. Don't eat too much. And save something for tomorrow.

COLOMBE.   Thank you so much, sir!

With a mocking little bow, PAUL *goes.*

Well?

JULIEN. Now our story begins. I'll never forget what you've given up for my sake.

COLOMBE. Oh, it's been too quick—I'm sure it's been too quick. It can't be the real thing, can it?

JULIEN. I think it is. And I think it will last.

He kisses her. She leans tightly against him.

COLOMBE (*a whisper*). My darling! . . . Now I'm sure of it . . . for always.

JULIEN. For always. . . . Not a second less.

They kiss, and
THE CURTAIN FALLS

180 C
47

WOLVERHAMPTON
PUBLIC LIBRARIES